ACKNOWLEDGMENTS

I am indebted to many whose knowledge has influenced me and enabled me to write this book. Previous writers on this subject are especially appreciated; the reading list in the appendix represents only a few of their works. I thank experts in the clothing and outdoors industries and in the public sector who were willing to share their knowledge and time with me. I particularly thank Jack Stephenson for his assistance in reviewing certain sections of the book and especially for providing the material on the vapor-barrier. I also thank REI, for allowing me to use their chart on insulation thickness; the American Alpine Club, for allowing me to use their library; likewise, the New York Public Library.

Special thanks go to Len David and Josh Weinstein for their assistance. Very special thanks go to Rita Fishman for her support and editing of the book. For the support and growth I received in the areas of creativity and productivity, I thank Werner Erhard and Robert Fritz. I also thank many friends, relatives and acquaintances who have given encouragement and support to my work. There also were people I met only once on a ski lift or knew through seminars who were enthusiastic about the book. Many a positive word meant more than they could have realized.

SECRETS *of* WARMTH

FOR COMFORT OR SURVIVAL

HAL WEISS

THE
MOUNTAINEERS

Published by
The Mountaineers
1001 SW Klickitat Way, Suite 201
Seattle, WA 98134

First edition 1988, second edition 1992 by Cloudcap
The Mountaineers Books: first printing 1998, second printing
1999

Published simultaneously in Great Britain by Cordee
3a DeMontfort Street, Leicester, England, LE1 7HD

Manufactured in the United States of America

Cover design by Jennifer Shontz
Cover photograph: Winter ski camp below Cathedral Peak, John
Muir Trail, Yosemite National Park, CA © 1993 Galen Rowell

Library of Congress Cataloging-in-Publication Data available

Printed on recycled paper

TABLE OF CONTENTS

PREFACE

While I personally have suffered only a few minor annoyances from the cold, I've always been interested in the subject. I've been disturbed whenever I've read about someone dying from the cold: the needless tragedy of a teenage girl dying while camping in Pennsylvania in April; the drowning of a tugboat crew when their ship sank under the weight of ice formed by stormy waves; the death of inexperienced climbers who were ignorant of weather conditions; the plight of skiers caught overnight in a chairlift. I've always felt many such deaths could have been avoided.

I've attempted here to provide enough information to make a real difference in a person's ability to keep warm, no matter what the activity or weather conditions. Experts differ on a number of issues about warmth, and I had to choose among various ideas. This book represents my opinions about the subject; I hope they are helpful to you.

In assessing any particular incidents, it was not my intent to judge or slight anyone, living or dead. I have examined the results of actions and decisions, with an accute awareness that second-guessing is easy in the comfort of a warm room.

1
WARMTH

Many people today spend most of their lives in comfortable artificial environments. They're shocked when circumstances force them to realize how vulnerable we've all become to the elemental forces of nature.

Paralyzing snow and ice storms shut off power by breaking power lines and overloading circuits, sometimes leaving major cities, even whole regions, without heat or hot water for days. Blizzards dump so much snow that traffic movement essentially stops. Cars get stuck on snowy highways; some of the people trapped in the cars are unable to survive the cold.

When severe weather continues for more than a few hours, many people get into serious trouble. Few motorists bother to carry emergency gear, except perhaps battery cables. Even in sub-freezing temperatures, most people dress just to get quickly from their car to their place of work, and they don't bother to bring along any additional warm clothing. Given our ability to prepare for cold weather, too many people get into trouble, even life-threatening trouble, when the weather turns stormy and cold. Reading about the casualties of storms isn't pleasant, but maybe it can open our eyes.

A friend once waited about an hour for a taxi on a very cold night. When her feet started to get really cold, she decided to walk home. By the time she reached her house, her feet were almost completely numb. As they thawed, she experienced excruciating pain and was frightened, conditions that persisted through most of the hours it took before her feet felt warm again. She got off with only a bad case of frostnip and no aftereffects. But had she been exposed to the cold twenty or thirty minutes longer, she probably would have suffered permanent frostbite and would have required immediate medical care, to say nothing of the discomfort of the long-term consequences of frostbite.

Sometimes it's misery for campers. A colleague of mine took his sons camping in cold weather. He hadn't done much camping and didn't know how to prepare or what to expect from the weather. He and his sons found out soon enough. The cold overwhelmed them and routed them out of their camp in the middle of the night. Their car was close by and they headed home, feeling miserable and cold. They experienced only frustration and inconvenience; other campers unprepared for the cold have experienced much worse, sometimes fatal, consequences.

WINTER STORMS

On February 10, 1983, one of the worst winter storms in four decades hit the East Coast. The storm dumped two to three feet of snow from the Carolinas through New England. Washington, Baltimore, Philadelphia and Trenton were virtually paralyzed. New York City was also nearly at a standstill. The temperature in New York was in the low 20s, but farther north in New Hampshire, the mercury plunged to $-12\,^{\circ}$F. Thirty buses were abandoned in the Brooklyn/Battery Tunnel, necessitating its closure. The Lincoln Tunnel also was blocked; about twenty people were stranded in it overnight. In New Jersey, cars were stuck all along the Garden State Parkway, stranding many people; authorities rescued 348 during the night and early morning. Another six-hundred motorists found shelter at a Red Cross headquarters in Frederick County, Maryland, where the snowfall was reportedly 35 inches. Cars were stranded on I-95 from Pennsylvania through New York, New Jersey and Connecticut. Who knows how many people suffered through that night!

In late January 1977, a winter storm paralyzed Buffalo, New York, for many days. Although the area is accustomed to snow, this particular storm was the worst in decades. By the time it was over, at least 23 people were dead because of the storm, and more than a hundred cases of serious frostbite were reported by area hospitals. At least six of those who died were stranded motorists who froze to death in their cars or in nearby snow banks. As a result of the same storm, five men in one car were frozen to death in Seneca County, Ohio.

The worst storm ever to hit Ohio came in January 1978. The Red Cross provided shelter for more than twenty thousand people. Another twelve hundred were sheltered by the National Guard. More than twenty thousand homes were without electricity. The most tragic result of the storm was discovered during the highway cleanup. As snowplows finally cleared the huge amounts of snow, it was discovered that fourteen stranded motorists had frozen to death.

The idea that today in our "civilized" society a person can leave home or work in a car and then *freeze to death* is unthinkable. We don't think about the possibility, and therefore we don't prepare for it. This is why people die. Preparing for cold emergencies isn't difficult, but most people *don't know how.* Think of this: With a bit of knowledge, a stack of newspapers or a thick telephone book could save your life in extremely cold weather! — and not by burning!

Warmth

The Four Inns Walking Competition

In his booklet, *Hypothermia: Killer of the Unprepared,* Dr. Theodore G Lathrop wrote about the 1964 renewal of this famous walking race held on the English moors. In 1964, competitors experienced heavy rains, sleet, snow, temperatures down to 35°F and winds up to 38 mph. Of 240 original participants, only 22 finished the race; three men died from hypothermia, and five others had close calls with hypothermic death. A study of the effects of wet, windy conditions on the clothing worn by the victims pointed up that under these weather conditions, only one-tenth of the original insulative value remained. The conclusion is clear: in addition to having adequate insulation, it is essential to have windproof, waterproof outer clothing for adequate protection from the elements.

Death in the Mountains

Almost all famous mountains, such as Mount Hood, Mount McKinley, Mount Rainier and Mount Washington, have grim histories of climbers dying from hypothermia. Over the years, many people have been caught without adequate protection in the severe weather conditions that can arise suddenly in the mountains. Climbers and campers sometimes are fooled by pleasant, even hot, weather at the base of the mountain; later they get caught in a downpour or a snowstorm only a few hundred feet higher. This happened on the slopes of Ixtacihuatl in Mexico in 1969. A group of 29 schoolboys started to climb to the 17,342' summit. Before they were much higher than their starting elevation, they were hit by a storm. Whiteout conditions (usually created by a combination of flat lighting and dense fog on snow-covered terrain, which makes it impossible to determine if one is on a level surface or a very steep slope) prevented them from retreating. Twelve boys died from the cold.

Similar accidents have occurred on Mount Washington in New Hampshire. With an elevation of only a little over six thousand feet, this mountain wouldn't seem to be an imposing threat. But its summit has been whipped by some of the highest winds recorded anywhere in the world; its wind meter once broke off while registering 214 mph. On October 2, 1987, it was 70°F and sunny at the base of Mount Washington while a harsh snowstorm raged at the summit, where the temperature was only 15°F. A group of Boy Scouts once started to hike up the mountain dressed only in shorts and short sleeve shirts; they took along no additional clothing. The weather suddenly turned very cold, and a snowstorm hit them. A number of the Scouts died. There many markers on Mount Washington commemorating such accidents.

Secrets of Warmth

The Mount Hood Disaster

On May 12, 1986, a group of nineteen people began a climb of 11,245' Mount Hood in Oregon. They were part of a local school's "outdoor" program and consisted of students, a few teachers and two experienced leaders. The climb is relatively simple when done under fair weather conditions. Snow conditions, the weather, and lack of preparation for the conditions encountered turned this particular climb into a survival situation; nine people, including the leader, died from hypothermia, and one student had to have part of his legs amputated.

There were a number of decisions made on the day of the climb which, with hindsight, may now be considered to have caused the tragic results. Rather than questioning any of these, it seems more useful to see what lessons may be learned from those who survived. Six people had turned back within the first two hours after the climb began, and another two weren't feeling well. Most of the climbers were by then cold-fatigued; the weather had already turned bad (visibility was only fifty feet). Eventually, one of the student's symptoms of hypothermia became severe enough for the group to stop to try to rewarm him. They spent a half hour trying to rewarm him by placing him in a sleeping bag with another climber and by giving him hot drinks. In other circumstances this might have been appropriate; here it meant everyone else was losing valuable body heat in the storm. A much better tactic would have been to have other members of the group start to dig a snow cave in case conditions got worse.

The rewarming was not as successful as they would have wished, yet they had to move on before everyone else got any colder. What they, as well as many other winter travelers, didn't realize is that IT TAKES A MUCH GREATER AMOUNT OF ENERGY TO REWARM A PERSON THAN IT DOES TO STAY WARM IN THE FIRST PLACE. Although the hot drinks helped, the heat that was already lost by the student probably could have boiled twenty cups of water. Given the conditions, I believe it would have taken at least three to five hours to fully rewarm that student, if they were already sheltered from the storm.

As they continued their descent, storm conditions grew worse, route finding was extremely difficult and the condition of the group was rapidly deteriorating. The decision was finally made to dig in. There was only one shovel in the group and the cave that was made was about the size of a three-man tent. One tarp covered the floor and thirteen people tried to fit in. They had to pile on top of one another, most had their backs against the snow. Their shovel was lost during the night as they were trying to keep the cave entrance open from the blowing snow. In the morning the assistant leader (who was now the de facto leader; the original leader was severely hypothermic) decided to try to go for help. He and a student volunteer eventually struggled down the mountain to Timberline Lodge.

By this time a rescue effort had already been organized, and teams started out to find the remaining climbers. The weather got so bad that rescuers had to dig a snow cave for their own survival. Three bodies were found the next day. The cave with the missing climbers was not found until yet another day went by. It was by then under five feet of new snow. Of the eight people still in the cave, only two survived. These two had been at or near the top of the pile of bodies, largely insulated from direct contact with the snow.

The leader of the group had attempted the climb about eighteen times before. He had made the decision to turn back on about two out of three of those attempts, due to weather or the condition of the group. Why the decision to turn back was not made at the appropriate time on this attempt is impossible to know for sure. It is thought by some that the leader himself was, perhaps, hypothermic long before anyone realized. This is quite plausible. One of the most insidious effects of hypothermia is poor judgment.

The tragedy on Mount Hood received extensive national media attention even as the drama unfolded. The full story, and some possible reasons for the failure of the climb, were detailed only months later by an investigative team of renowned climbers. Their report received very little attention except in the local press. Much of the public was left only with a general impression that winter-type climbing conditions can be dangerous; little information was given to show how the outcome could have been different.

SUCCESSFUL WINTER TRAVEL

When a winter trip or climb is well planned and appropriate equipment is used, the results are usually vastly different from the emergencies that occur when people are caught unprepared. When we prepare for the conditions we expect, we almost automatically include a little something extra for the unexpected. Then if the unexpected does happen, we may suffer some discomfort, but we won't face a life-or-death situation. Planning for the cold pays off whether we're traveling two blocks to go shopping, two hundred miles to go skiing or five thousand miles to the Himalayas. Here are some examples of adventures in extreme conditions:

The Steger Expedition

The 1986 Steger Expedition to the North Pole is a prime example of the triumph of good planning and the use of good insulation. An eight-person team departed from Ward Hunt Island in Canada's Northwest Territories on March 8, 1986; they reached the North Pole on May 2. The team used forty nine dogs for their eight sleds (each carrying a thousand pounds) and travelled three hundred difficult miles without any resupply. Average temperatures they encountered were between –20° to –40°F, but during the first week or so, they experienced temperatures down to –71°F (without considering the wind-chill factor). Their clothing system consisted of: *Hollofil II* socks; *Thermolite* boot liners; *Thermax*-lined mukluks with leather bottoms (the bottoms were later replaced by *Cordura*); an underwear layer of *Thermax*; a polar one-piece suit (made by Wilderness Experience) with *Thermoloft* insulation in the body area, *Thermolite* insulation in the arm and leg areas and a *Thermax* lining; and, on top of this, a *Cordura* shell suit for protection from the wind and the sharp ice. An additional five pound *Quallofil* parka (made by North Face) was used during periods of inactivity. Their sleeping bags were one-foot thick, weighed fifteen pounds and used *Quallofil* for the insulation. These special bags were made with a snorkle hood (an extension above the bag) to provide a warmed layer of air next to the face.

In addition to planning their personal insulation, the team also planned their travel route, timing, food and fuel supply. Team members also prepared their bodies through exercises appropriate for the hard traveling they would have to endure. In short, they prepared well for the task they set out to accomplish; they could not have hoped for a successful result without such preparation. *Good preparation doesn't guarantee success, but the lack of good preparation invites failure.* Given the temperatures and the wind that members of the Steger Expedition had to endure, if the team members' insulation system had failed, they almost certainly would have lost their lives. When we consider that many people have died from the cold in temperatures *more than a hundred degrees higher* than the Steger Expedition experienced, it becomes clear that lack of preparation and/or knowledge is usually at fault. It's also obvious if the expedition was in extreme conditions, then the preparation required for the much more gentle weather we normally face is possible — and probably easier — than we imagine.

Others Who Stretched the Limits

The Swan Expedition started on November 3, 1985, and reached the South Pole on January 11, 1986. The three-man team travelled approximately nine hundred miles on skis, pulling sledges that carried their only food and supplies. The expedition retraced the route of the tragic 1911 trip of Captain Robert F Scott, whose team died while returning from the Pole. The Swan Expedition was well prepared, physically and mentally, and carried sufficient cold weather gear. They were able to survive two injuries during the trek, in spite of having to travel many long days in 20°F weather.

In 1980 Reinhold Messner reached an altitude of 29,028' on foot. That's right, he was at the top of Mount Everest, alone and without oxygen. He, too, was obviously well prepared and had enough cold weather clothing to make it there and back alive. Messner had performed the same amazing feat two years before with Peter Habeler, but came back to do it again solo; he changed the course of mountain climbing. More important for our present purposes, he showed what is possible in cold weather travel, even in the highest altitude.

2
THE BASICS

HOW THE BODY REACTS TO COLD

The human body functions best at about 98.6°F; its internal organs can tolerate only a small deviation from this "normal" temperature. The body uses various mechanisms to maintain temperature:

In a sense, the body is very much like an automobile's cooling system, with circulating blood acting as the coolant. Heat is generated primarily in the muscles and internal organs, which warm the blood passing through them. That blood then flows throughout the body and transfers its heat to cooler parts of the body; the heat eventually escapes through the skin and into the environment. Here's an important (and useful) point: **If you keep any part of your body warmer, the extra warmth will be circulated through your entire body.** It's especially helpful to keep your neck and head warm, because you can lose more than half of your heat flow through this area. Thus the old axiom of outdoorsmen: "Put on your hat if your feet are cold."

To some extent, the body can regulate its rate of metabolism; that is, it can increase the rate its cells oxidize fuel even without an increase in the body's level of activity. This generates heat, but it also drains the energy stores of the body and can lead to the early onset of exhaustion. This ability is probably more valuable for people with very good endurance who can replenish their energy more quickly than those in poor shape. In other words, people who recover very quickly from physical exertion would also recover quickly from an increase in metabolic rate.

Another way the body regulates its temperature is to open (dilate) blood vessels in the extremities (arms, legs, hands, feet, skin) when it is too warm and constrict them when it is too cold. This mechanism, called vasoconstriction, works by reducing the blood flow (and therefore also the heat flow) to the extremities, thus allowing the extremities to cool to a lower temperature than the body-core temperature. Since the laws of physics dictate that the rate of heat transfer between two masses (you and the air) is directly related to the difference in their temperatures, by lowering the temperature of the skin, the body lowers the rate of heat loss to the air. Next in order of blood-flow constriction is the area just beneath the skin and then the deeper muscle tissue. This turns the body's outer shell (the mantle) into an insulator which helps the body maintain its core temperature. This automatic mechanism of constricting blood vessels does not work in the neck and head because the brain always needs a constant supply of blood. This is one reason so much heat can be lost through the head and neck if they are not well insulated. When the blood flow is shifted from the outer mantle of the body, another heat-saving effect results. The blood vessels that carry the blood away from the extremities are closer together than they are in the outer mantle. This creates a heat-exchange effect. Blood in veins traveling close to arteries with relatively warmer blood is warmed by that flow, and the warm arterial flow is cooled by the veinous flow. So blood returning to the inner core is warmer, and blood going to the outer mantle has less heat to lose. Occasionally, blood flow through constricted areas will be returned for short periods to try to maintain life in these areas. This action will not continue if the core temperature gets too low. The tenacity with which the body will use vasoconstriction is truly amazing. It will go so far as to sacrifice the limbs if necessary to maintain the core temperature.

A fourth mechanism the body uses to retain heat creates what we commonly call goose pimples. A chill felt on the skin will cause hair follicles to stand on end, and tiny air pockets will form under the skin, giving the skin a pimpled irregular configuration we're familiar with. These physical changes result in an increased ability to maintain the body's warmth, although not to any great degree in humans. The hair standing on end traps more dead air, as does the irregular skin surface. The tiny pockets under the skin are dead air (which is the best insulation, next to a perfect vacuum). The mechanism of goose pimples (or goose bumps) is much more effective for animals that are feathered, extremely hairy or fur-bearing. It can increase their effective insulation layer many fold; by comparison, it does little for us.

Shivering is another regulatory device of the body. When the body senses that the core temperature is dropping below normal, it causes involuntary contractions in various muscles. This process is actually most useful as an alarm system. As soon as you start to shiver, you should know that you've let your body temperature drop too low and you'd better do something about it immediately. Get out of the weather and into shelter, increase your body insulation, take over muscle movement yourself consciously — or do all three things, if necessary, to stop the involuntary shivering. The body knows that by forcing muscles to contract it can generate heat, the resultant shivering is not an efficient process. You can do a much better job by working your muscles consciously: by doing isometric exercises. Isometrics are done by pitting one set of muscles against other muscles or immovable objects. For instance, if your hands are cold, clenching your fists for five to ten seconds and releasing them for the same time will begin to generate heat in them in a few minutes. If your whole body is cold, the isometrics should involve more and larger muscle groups. But don't strain your muscles; that can cause pain or cramping. Windmilling of the arms, which people sometimes do to warm up, should be avoided because the pumping action functions like a bellows. It displaces warm air in clothing, and colder outside air comes through the neck, wrist and waist areas. By windmilling, you can easily lose more heat from your insulation than you build up in your body. Isometrics are much more efficient. All of the body's mechanisms together, however, can't keep our unclothed body warm enough even in mildly cold weather. So, we have to protect ourselves from the cold with an artificial micro-environment which is our clothing system.

HOW THE BODY GAINS HEAT

The basic method the human body uses to obtain its heat energy is by metabolizing the food it consumes. The food is transformed into fuel that is usable to the cells and is oxidized (or burned) by the cells. Most of the heat given off by the cells is from internal organs and muscles. Muscles are only about one-third efficient. This means that only one-third of the energy they produce is in the form of mechanical tension; the other two-thirds is in the form of waste heat. Of course, "waste heat" is a thermodynamic term, and the heat obviously is not wasted if our body needs it in a cold environment. The sun can provide a small amount of warmth, especially if the outer layer of your clothing is dark, since dark colors absorb the sun's radiation better than light colors. Unfortunately, dark colors also are more efficient in radiating heat. Since there are few hours of sunlight in winter, you probably will have a net heat loss if you wear a dark outer shell. A fire also can provide heat, if built properly. But neither the sun nor fire can be relied upon for warmth. The sun may be obscured by clouds for days, even weeks, at a time, and one can easily be caught in conditions that make building a fire impossible. The food you metabolize can provide your body with reliable heat; frequent rest can conserve it; and your clothing system can retain it long enough for your body to maintain its crucial temperature of 98.6°F. The basic metabolic rate for the average man is approximately 70 calories per hour during sleep; it can be more than seven times that much during heavy work or exercise. In any extended outdoor activity, more food should be eaten to make up for the extra work and cold temperatures. The food consumed does not have to be hot. Hot food provides few extra calories compared with the fuel value of the food itself. Hot drinks can add a little warmth and should be taken if extra warmth is needed but, again, this doesn't provide as much heat as the caloric value of the food.

HOW THE BODY LOSES HEAT

There are five basic ways the body loses heat to the external environment:

Heat Loss from Conduction

This involves the transfer of heat energy from a warmer object to a colder one in direct physical contact. Energy always travels from a higher energy state to a lower one, and the warmer object is the one at a higher energy state. So, although it may seem as though we become cold from touching something which feels colder, we actually are giving up our heat energy to it. Some objects conduct heat better than others. If you have ever touched cold metal in winter, you know how quickly your fingers become numb. In general, metals are excellent conductors, and the ones that conduct electricity best, such as copper and aluminum, also conduct heat best. That's why you'll see these two metals used on the bottom of cooking pots; they conduct the heat efficiently to the food being cooked. It's a good idea not to touch metal with the bare skin in the winter since we want to conserve heat. Even metal zippers are avoided by most winter outdoorsmen, with nylon being the preferred material.

Conduction between the ground and shoes, boots or any foot covering is one reason it can be difficult to keep feet warm. Heat loss through conduction can also be a problem for your bottom when sitting on cold ground, a cold stadium bench, a cold ski lift or snow. Usually, the denser the material, the faster it transfers heat. Since water is much more dense than air, immersion in cold water is much more dangerous than being in cold air. Your body gives up heat to the water 240 times faster than it does to air. Materials that are poor conductors of heat are called insulators. The best insulator would be no material at all, or a perfect vacuum. That's why a vacuum Thermos bottle maintains liquids at their original temperature, whether hot or cold, over a long period of time. The next best insulator is a still gas such as air, but air tends to move a lot. So to keep it from moving, we fragment it into small packets. This is what your clothing actually does when it is well designed as winter wear. **The real insulation in winter clothing is air**. This point will be repeated later. Another top insulator is plastic foam, like a Styrofoam cup which keeps your hand comfortable when it's only about an eighth of an inch away from boiling hot coffee. Other good insulators are fibrous materials such as wood, animal skins and clothes, both natural and man-made (see Chapter 3, Materials). An insulator protects you from cold by slowing the rate of heat flow away from you; that is, because it's a poor conductor. The material which fragments air into tiny pockets in clothing comprises only about one percent of the clothing's volume; the rest is air. Conduction through this material is only a small percentage of total conduction. In well designed winter clothing, conduction of heat through air is the main source of heat loss, with radiation less than half as much and convection inside the garment about ten percent as much as air conduction.

Heat Loss from Convection

Convection is the transfer of heat by the movement of a fluid or gas. Air is our best insulator, and all clothing systems try to retain dead (immobile) air. Our bodies warm the air molecules close to us by conduction and radiation. This warmed air (which is therefore less dense and lighter) tends to rise in relation to the air molecules farther away from us. The warmed molecules are continuously replaced with the cooler ones; this action is called natural convection. The same process can and does occur between the thin inner layers of our clothing (underwear and shirts) and the outer layers (thick jacket or coat). The warmer air rises, escapes near the neck and is replaced by colder air coming in at the waist or sleeves. This natural convection between insulation layers is often referred to as the "chimney effect." It can be cause considerable heat loss if left unchecked. If we move our arms and thus force air through our clothes, the warmer inner air is replaced with cooler outside air; this bellows type action is called forced convection. When the wind is blowing, it continuously moves away the layer of air next to us; this also is forced convection. Up to a point, the stronger the wind, the greater the heat loss. This is why wind-chill charts were developed (see page 36); they give us an idea of the temperature our skin would feel at different wind velocities. Under some conditions, convection can be a major source of heat loss, such as when you are not well insulated and your outer layer of clothing is not windproof.

Heat Loss from Radiation

All matter containing thermal energy (including humans) constantly radiates a small portion of that energy. It is transmitted mostly in the form of infrared radiation. No medium is necessary for transferring this energy; it can travel in a vacuum. Infrared is one of the wavelengths on which we receive the sun's energy which warms the planet Earth. The Earth also radiates energy into space, but since the sun is at a much higher energy level than Earth, Earth receives more energy than it radiates. Earth's radiation is most noticeable to us on clear nights, especially in winter. On such nights, radiation has a direct path into space, resulting in ground temperatures that are ten to twenty degrees lower than on cloudy nights.

Conversely, cloud cover reflects much of the radiant heat back to earth, so cloudy nights mean temperatures stay higher. In warm temperatures, when you wear very little clothing, 50 to 65 percent of your body heat is lost through radiation. In cold climates, when you wear more clothing, the radiant energy of your body heats the air in your clothing system (if well designed), and the major source of heat loss will be conduction through the air (if convection is handled well by your clothing).

As the name indicates, radiant heaters also work through radiation. A heating element receives electrical energy to that point at which it emits the most infrared radiation. The warmth you feel from these heaters travels directly to you and does not heat the room first. Ordinary heaters (including water-filled radiators) heat the air in a room by convection and radiation, and this then warms the occupants. Loss of heat by radiation becomes noticeable when you're in a warm room, and you're close to a cold wall or window. That part of your body facing the cold wall feels the coldness without actually touching the wall. Ordinarily, most things in a room are at the same temperature, so they radiate about the same amount. If an item is much colder than its surroundings, it won't radiate the same amount of heat. So, the cold wall is radiating much less heat to you than you are to it. The cold you feel is the net loss of energy from the part of you facing the wall.

Since infrared radiation is just below the visible light spectrum, you can't see it leave your body. You just feel colder. Radiation can be a major source of heat loss under certain conditions. If you are poorly insulated in very cold conditions, your major heat loss will be through radiation (and convection if there's any wind). Also, if your body is well insulated but your head isn't, (for instance, if you're in a sleeping bag without a hood), you can lose more than three-quarters of your body's heat through radiation and convection from your head.

Heat Loss from Evaporation

The three forms of matter we're familiar with are solid, liquid and gas. Many substances can appear in these different states at different times. Water can be liquid or solid (ice) or a gas (water vapor, or steam). The state it appears in depends on its energy level. If you add enough energy to ice, it turns to water; if you add enough energy to water, it turns to water vapor. To understand how much heat is needed to evaporate water from your skin, consider that it takes one BTU (252 calories) to raise the temperature of one pound of water by 1°F; if you want to evaporate that pound of water, you must multiply that amount of energy a thousand-fold. For perspiration to evaporate from our skin, clearly it must gain a lot of energy. It's not going to get much energy from the cold air, so it's our skin that loses heat energy to cause the evaporation. That's welcome in the summer when we need the cooling. In winter, however, when we're trying to conserve heat, this evaporation can drain an amazing amount of heat from us. This explains an old axiom of winter travelers: "Don't sweat!"

There are two types of perspiration; sensible and insensible. Sensible perspiration (noticeable) is ordinary sweat caused by overheating. Insensible perspiration (not noticeable) is the moisture your skin has to produce to maintain the health of the skin. The humidity level at the skin surface has to be 75–100 percent; otherwise, the skin would dry out and crack, leaving the body more vulnerable to germs, chemicals and sunlight damage. Unlike sensible perspiration, this moisturizing of the skin is a continual process. Since cold air is dry, skin moisture is continually evaporating and is, therefore, an ongoing source of heat loss. A winter camper can easily lose two or more pounds of water a night from insensible perspiration in an ordinary sleeping bag, and he can lose the same amount or more during the day. This is why winter travelers are urged to drink lots of water; they lose a lot of water without ever noticing the loss.

Heat Loss from Respiration

Breathing also causes heat loss. It's actually a combination of evaporation and convection, but I list it separately because it's such a significant form of heat loss. When we inhale cold, dry air, our nasal passages and sinus areas heat the incoming air and increase its humidity to almost 100 percent so that the bronchial tubes and lungs are protected; dry air would cause spasms in bronchial and lung tissue. When we exhale, we lose much of the heat and moisture we've given to air we inhaled. Thus, we lose heat in two ways: by the heat we have to produce to warm the incoming air and then by the heat contained in the water vapor lost when we exhale. (Remember, the body evaporated the water to moisturize the inhaled air, and evaporation requires a lot of heat.)

In *Hypothermia, Death by Exposure,* Dr. William Forgey notes that at 0°F, an average man's convective heat loss due to warming of incoming air is approximately 18 calories per hour. The heat loss from evaporation to moisturize this air is about 24 calories per hour. Thus, the total heat loss is 42 calories per hour. Now compare this with the average basal metabolic rate of 70 calories per hour and you can see that **just by sitting still at 0°F, you are losing more than half of your body's entire heat production just by breathing!** Under normal circumstances this loss is compensated for, but it's still significant. Some animals use this mechanism in warm weather as their main method of cooling: such as a dog's panting. In very cold dry air, in high altitudes and during heavy exertion, the amount of heat lost by breathing is enormous. In a survival situation, this loss must be slowed or survival time may be greatly shortened. Some ways to deal with respiration heat loss (as well as the other forms) are discussed in the next section and in the section on survival.

BLOCKING THE PATHS OF HEAT LOSS

Handling Conduction

The way to protect against heat loss through conduction is by insulation, and the insulation we use is air. Air is a poor conductor of heat, so it slows the heat loss. But if we don't seal the air with other materials, it is rapidly displaced with colder air by convection. So we package the air in our clothing systems, and this becomes our insulation. The material of our clothing makes up about 1 percent of the volume; the other 99 percent is air. This means that the value of the material itself as an insulator is not very important, but what is crucial is how well it contains air. Air inside our clothing is great insulation. The outside air is helping to make us cold. So the thicker our clothing layers, the more air there is for insulation, and the warmer we are.

THICKNESS = WARMTH.

The most rapid heat loss by conduction occurs when we are in direct contact with solids or liquids. This ususally happens when we are standing, sitting, kneeling, lying down or gripping something, causing some part of our body to compress the insulation around it. If the insulation is compressed to half its original thickness, it will protect us only half as much from the cold. Therefore, to be effective against conduction to solids, insulation should be relatively incompressible. Various foam materials are best for this type of insulation. Many boot and shoe soles now are being made out of lighter foams (such as those used in running shoes) which contain more air and therefore are warmer. Older style soles made out of heavier rubber or leather are much colder.

People who work outside in winter and stand in one place for a long time (such as street vendors) lose a great deal of heat through conduction to the cold ground. I have often seen vendors lift one foot and then the other in an effort to keep their feet warm. If they could stand on a one or two inch thick piece of styrofoam insulation (perhaps a scrap thrown away from building construction), they could avoid the misery of cold feet. A stack of two or three Sunday newspapers would work nearly as well, just as long as the paper doesn't get wet. Tightly knit wool gloves are good for handling equipment such as cameras in cold weather, although much more effective neoprene gloves are now being sold in some camping stores. Neoprene is a closed-cell foam previously used primarily by skin divers. Even neoprene socks are available; they are much warmer than wool socks.

No knowlegeable winter camper would use a sleeping bag without a mattress or foam pad beneath it. If he or she did, the heat lost by conduction to the cold ground or snow (due to the body compressing the insulation on the underside of the bag) would cause the camper to have a miserably cold night and little, if any, sleep. The "popsicle" leaving the bag in the morning would not likely make that mistake again! Even when no sleeping bag is carried by a winter traveler, a closed-cell foam pad is an excellent piece of survival gear. In any kind of shelter, you're not likely to be standing for long, so you need protection from the cold ground or the snow. The increase in survival time could be days, not just hours, when a foam pad is used.

Handling Convection

Still air is the best insulation. Since convection is the motion of air, insulation breaks up air into small packets, and this greatly reduces its motion. Slow down the motion of air and you slow the rate of heat loss. Increase the amount of air captured by your insulation by increasing the *thickness* of your insulation, and you've also slowed the rate of heat loss. For a description of some of the best materials for insulation, see Chapter 3. To handle forced convection, such as the wind, insulation must be protected from the colder outside air pushing out the warmed insulated air. To accomplish this, the outer clothing layer surrounding the insulation should be very tightly knit. There should also be as few stitches as possible in this outer fabric. Putting a lot of decorative stitch lines into a coat or jacket can turn a good windproof fabric into an air-leaking sieve.

The bellows action of our movements, which causes air displacement, can be countered by using knit, form-fitting materials at the neck, wrists, ankles and waist areas. They should never fit so tightly as to impede blood circulation or their effect will be worse than the bellows action they prevent. Velcro material is adjustable for this purpose and allows better ventilation at wrists and ankles. A zipper can also allow some adjustability. Another method of handling forced convection from within, as well as natural convection of the "chimney effect," is to wear a loosely knit sweater which can take up much of the slack of a poorly draped jacket. The air pocket between you and your jacket, as well as the insulation of your jacket itself, may be ineffective without an internal wind block like a sweater. Also effective for this purpose is an elasticised waist for a jacket or shell, a drawcord at the waist or a device that goes by various names such as winddam, snow skirt, snow dam, etc. This is an extended piece of material that closes tightly around your waist and prevents snow and wind from entering under your jacket.

Handling Radiation

Radiation may be dealt with in two ways: by reflecting part of the radiated heat back to its source (you) and by reducing the radiation emission capability of your outer clothing layer. One way to reflect radiant heat is by having your insulating layer sufficiently thick so that there are enough fibers to reflect most of the infrared waves. This scatters the waves and warms the air inside your insulation, rather than having the heat travel directly out. The thickness required for this is about ¾ to 1 inch of insulation. Another way to reflect radiant heat is to use material, such as a metalized fabric, that is opaque to infrared waves. Some manufacturers now use radiative heat barriers (also known as radiant heat reflectors) in jackets and sleeping bags; this is not always cost-effective or weight-effective. As stated above, proper insulation (more than than ¾ inch) is sufficient to protect against this type of heat loss. My own field testing of radiant barrier gloves, commonly sold in ski shops, showed they lacked the capability to keep my hands warm.

At the opposite end of the scale is a thin insulation called *Thermal/RTM* which makes effective use of reflective material in a thin layer. The best use of a radiant heat reflector is in emergency gear. It is assumed that in emergency situations the available insulation is not thick enough to provide sufficient warmth; the amount of heat lost through radiation is therefore increased and radiant heat barriers are necessary. This is why vapor-barrier suits and space blankets sold as emergency gear are usually coated to reflect infrared waves back to the wearer.

The second basic method of handling radiation is to reduce the capability of your outermost layer (and possibly an inner layer near your body) to emit infrared radiation. Lighter colored cloth helps somewhat. The white outfits of ski troopers during WWII actually helped them stay a little warmer, although it was intended only as camouflage. One of the best materials for low-emission properties is a light-colored textile metalized with aluminum. Some garments use other low-emission coatings; one is the vapor barrier shirt made by Stephenson and another is *Thermal/RTM* insulation.

Handling Evaporation

To control heat loss through evaporation, both sensible and insensible perspiration must be considered. For sensible perspiration, or sweat, the answer is easy: **DON'T SWEAT!** Slow down your rate of activity, reduce the amount of insulation you're wearing, ventilate your insulation, or do some combination of the three. The first method, slowing down, is best because it conserves your energy and helps you avoid fatigue. At times when you can't slow down, reducing your insulation or venting (unzipping at the openings) is extremely important to prevent moisture buildup inside your insulation.

There is a fourth method to control heat loss from sweat, and that's by using a vapor-barrier under your insulation; this will be described in detail in Chapter 3. For insensible perspiration, neither slowing the rate of activity nor reducing insulation does any good because a certain amount of moisture must be produced continuously to protect the skin. Compensating for this by increasing the insulation and allowing a small amount of venting is probably the only way to prevent moisture buildup in a breathable clothing system. In this case, you're trading off some convective and evaporative losses to prevent worse evaporative losses in the future. This is of some value, but there's a better way. Use of a vapor barrier is the only really effective way to stop evaporative heat loss from insensible perspiration as well as sensible perspiration.

Handling Respiration

You can't stop breathing, so heat loss through respiration is inevitable. You can, however, slow this kind of heat loss significantly when necessary. Under normal conditions it isn't necessary, but for people with respiratory problems, for elderly persons who must travel in bitter cold or for travelers caught in cold emergencies, decreasing the loss of heat and moisture from respiration is very important. One effective method is to breathe through either a mask or a few layers of porous material placed over your mouth and nose. Much of your breath's moisture (at almost 98.6°F, it's warm moisture) is trapped between the fibers of the cloth mask when you exhale. When you inhale, this moisture both warms and moisturizes the incoming air. A commercial product made just for this purpose is the 3M-brand *Air-Warming Mask*. It looks like a dust mask and weighs only about half an ounce. Does it work? Yes! An advertising claim for it states that in an environment with temperature of 20°F and humidity of only 10 percent, use of the mask causes inhaled air to register temperature of 60°F and 95 percent humidity. That's a big claim, but probably close to the real figures.

The only time I actually used an air-warming mask was in a test some years ago while skiing. This particular model was plastic with multiple metal screen inserts. (I've never seen it sold since, but it may still be available.) The air temperature was near zero. My immediate reaction was pleasant surprise at how much more comfortable it was to breathe with the mask than without it. When I was without the mask, the air felt cold and rough on my throat. When I wore the mask, the air was much warmer, and it didn't hurt to breathe. Some face-warming masks used by skiers, such as those made of neoprene, accomplish a little of this air-warming action in addition to keeping the face warmer. As noted in the previous section on heat loss, through respiration you can lose more than half the heat produced by your basal metabolic rate. An air-warming mask costs very little, weighs only half an ounce, is not bulky and saves a lot of heat. So for emergency planning, as they say: "Don't leave home without it!"

Another way of conserving heat lost by respiration is the snorkle hood used on some winter parkas. This type of hood covers the head and neck completely and extends about six inches in front of the face, forming a tunnel five or six inches in diameter; this is sometimes capped off with a fur surround in front to prevent snow buildup. This tunnel creates in front of your face an air space which cannot be completely dislodged by the wind without some time lag. Your breath mixes with this air and warms it before you inhale. So the hood has the double benefit of protecting your face from the wind and pre-warming the air. A disadvantage is loss of peripheral vision.

WHAT IS HEAT?

Heat is a form of energy. Heat energy results from the vibrational energy of atoms and molecules; the faster these vibrations, the hotter a material is, or the more heat energy it contains. All matter, including our bodies, has heat energy.

How Hot It Is!

One way to measure heat is by comparing a substance's molecular vibrational rate with a known scale. We do this by putting the substance to be measured in contact with a column of fluid (such as mercury in a thermometer). If the substance is hotter than the fluid in the column, the faster molecules of the hotter substance speed up the slower molecules of the fluid. The molecules of the fluid, now vibrating faster, bounce off each other harder and more often. The molecular collisions in the fluid push the molecules farther apart and expand the fluid. We then read the height of that expanded fluid in a column and thus get the temperature of the substance we're measuring. The reverse occurs if the substance being measured is colder than the measuring fluid; a thermometer's mercury would contract and register a lower temperature. The column of fluid is graduated in units called degrees. On the Fahrenheit scale, the temperature at which water freezes is 32 degrees, and there are 180 degree divisions up to the point at which water boils at 212 degrees (at sea-level atmospheric pressure). These two reference points are zero and 100 degrees, respectively, on the Celsius scale. The imaginary point where all vibration would stop is known as absolute zero C and –460°F.

How Much There Is!

Since heat is a form of energy, it may be thought of in units that scientists use for measuring energy. The ones normally used to measure heat energy are the British thermal unit (BTU), calorie (cal) and kilogram-calorie (kcal). By definition, one calorie is the quantity of heat which must be supplied to one gram of water to raise its temperature by one degree Celsius. The kilogram-calorie, which equals 1000 calories, is the amount of heat needed to raise 1000 grams of water by one degree Celsius. The British thermal unit (BTU) is the amount of heat needed to raise one pound of water one degree Fahrenheit. To convert: one BTU equals 252 cal, or 0.252 kcal. It may seem boring to know how much heat it takes to make a bit of water one degree hotter. But if we add another factor, time, to the measurements, they become more useful.

How Quickly it Moves!

It usually takes about five minutes to boil a pot of water. You can't just add so many calories and poof! the water boils instantly. It takes time for the heat to be transferred from a heat source to the water. Likewise for us; it takes time for our bodies to produce heat, and it takes time to transfer (or lose) that heat to the environment. So we are more interested in the amount of heat produced, or lost, per unit of time; that is, the rate of heat transfer. The units of measurement used here are BTU/hr, kcal/min, kcal/hr, cal/hr, etc.

HEAT AND THE HUMAN BODY THERMAL EQUILIBRIUM

Our body cells function best at about 98.6°F. If this thermal energy level is increased just a few degrees (to, say, between 102° and 106°F), the chemical reactions in our cells and organs start to break down and we (almost literally) burn out and die. On the other hand, if our thermal energy level goes down a few degrees (to, say, about 96°F), we get into the first stages of hypothermia (subnormal body temperature; see Chapter 7). Again, the cells begin to function poorly, and if the energy level continues to go down, systems break down and death is the result.

Our bodies are living engines. The food we eat is oxidized (or burned) in our cells, and this produces energy in such various forms as electrical, chemical, mechanical and heat. Any energy the body produces which is not used chemically or mechanically is usually transferred to our surrounding environment in the form of heat. This is part of a process that provides thermal equilibrium; that is, it maintains our thermal energy level at 98.6°F

HEAT IN = HEAT OUT.

If your body is producing 70 calories per hour while you sleep, then you must get rid of 70 calories every hour or your temperature will rise. If your body is producing 200 calories per hour while you're walking, then you want to get rid of 200 calories per hour. In other words, you want heat produced to equal heat transferred to the environment. Your heat in, or heat produced by your body, is your basal metabolic rate (resting rate) plus the heat produced by your physical activity. If you are running, swimming, chopping wood, etc., your rate of heat production will depend on your particular activity and your particular body. Your control here is the rate at which you engage in the activity. If you slow down your rate of activity, you also slow your rate of heat production. Another example of a way you can control heat production is if you are stranded in a cold place and are sitting still, you can increase your heat production by consciously using muscles you don't really need to use; that is, by doing isometric exercises.

THE HEAT TRANSFER EQUATION

Heat-out, or heat transferred to the environment, usually depends to a large extent on conduction. Heat transfer can be described by the equation:

$$Q/T = K \times A \times (t1 - t2) / L$$

In words, the equation states: Heat-out per unit of time equals conductivity constant times area times temperature difference divided by thickness.

What Does the Equation Tell Us?

Q/T = The rate at which heat is being lost in BTUs per hour. This is the body heat loss we're trying to minimize.

K = The constant rate of heat conductivity of your insulation. During WWII, the US Army at its labs in Natwick, Mass., determined that the value of K was constant for almost all normal insulations. (The only exceptions are the micro-fibers and foams.)

A = The surface area of your body in square feet. The quantity of body surface is relatively constant for each individual. However, if you're in a survival situation, you can tuck your arms and legs into your body and reduce the surface area from which heat is being lost and thereby slow the rate of loss. Likewise with a group of people. If they huddle close together, they effectively reduce the area facing the environment and lower the rate of heat loss (This is also why mittens are warmer than gloves).

$t1 - t2$ = The temperature difference (in degrees F) between your skin and the outside air. The temperature at your skin is a quantity you want to keep constant, and the temperature outside is variable but not in your control. The equation tells us that heat loss is directly related to this temperature difference. As the difference becomes larger, which is to say, as the outside temperature goes lower, you lose heat more quickly.

L = The thickness (in inches) of your insulating layer, specifically the distance between you and the cold environment. Thickness has an inverse relationship to the rate of heat loss; this means that as your insulation gets thicker, you lose heat more slowly. **This is where your real control lies!** Simply put: you increase the **thickness** of your insulation until the **rate of heat loss** goes down to reach equilibrium with the **rate of heat production** of your body. This is most easily done by adding layers of clothing.

WHAT IS MEANT BY WARMTH; HOW IS IT MEASURED?

We think of an article of clothing as being warm if it keeps us warm. The warmth of a garment may be considered as its ability to hold heat. In other words, the more heat it can hold over time, the more slowly it transfers heat away from us and the warmer the garment is. Insulation has the job of slowing the rate of heat transfer. When engineers speak about home insulations they refer to R-values. This is a measure of thermal resistance per unit of thickness (an inch) and is derived from a form of the heat transfer equation:

R = (temperature difference) × (area) × (time) / (amount of heat transferred).

If the system of measurement uses degrees F, square feet, hours and BTUs (for amount of heat), then the unit of resistance is called the R-value.

During initial research on the insulating value of clothing, researchers created a standard of comparison. The standard value taken was the amount of clothing it takes to keep an average man comfortable in an indoor environment at 70°F with no wind. This thickness was called one Clo, and it turned out to be roughly the thickness of a normal business suit. The Clo and the R-value are both measured in the same units and are convertible from one to the other. If you multiply the Clo by .88 you get the R-value; if you multiply R by 1.136 you get the Clo.

Although Clo never became widely known to the public, the R-value did. The energy shortage of the early 1970s made many people aware of the R-value of the insulation in their homes. The higher the R-value, the slower the heat transfer and, therefore, the less money spent on fuel for heating. Being more widely known, the R-value may be better used than Clo for comparing insulations, including those for clothing. An even better way to compare insulations is by the inch. This applies only to those insulations which are very close in R-value, which means most insulations. The only exceptions are the micro-fibers such as *Thermolite,*

Thinsulate, Eizac, etc., and foam insulations such as *Thermal/RTM;* even these insulations vary only in their capacity to slow heat loss when they are thin. For temperatures below zero F, the thickness of the micro-fibers needed would be almost as thick as ordinary insulations. As the micro-fibers approach the thickness of regular insulations, their total R-value gets somewhat closer to regular insulations; they also will be heavier. Most normal insulation materials — such as polyesters (whether short-staple or long-fiber), down, wool, piles, fleece, etc. — are fairly close in thermal resistance for each inch of thickness.

HOW MUCH INSULATION?

How do we know how much insulation we need to stay warm in a given condition? This question is difficult to answer because of the many variables involved. We can get a good approximation by making some assumptions about the variables. We start by assuming an average individual in good health and good physical condition and then test to see what amount of insulation would keep that person warm under different temperatures. We can then add or subtract according to particular circumstances. Easier still is to let the folks in the testing labs do it for us. The Army Quartermaster labs in Natick, Mass., came out with figures for the amount of insulation, in inches, required for various temperatures and different energy outputs:

AMOUNT OF INSULATION

Effective Temp.	Sleeping	Light Work	Heavy Work
+40°F.	1.5″	0.8″	0.20″
+20°F.	2.0″	1.0″	0.27″
0°F.	2.5″	1.3″	0.35″
–20°F.	3.0″	1.6″	0.40″
–40°F.	3.5″	1.9″	0.48″
–50°F.	4.0″	2.1″	0.52″

The Basics

This chart *must* be used thoughtfully and with caution. The temperature refers to the effective temperature without wind; humidity is not considered, nor is altitude. Various physical parameters can affect us: physical condition, mental attitude, food and water intake, metabolic rate, fatigue level, etc. Also, this chart assumes an equal thickness of insulation covering the entire body; such a circumstance is extremely rare. Finally, while the Army may be concerned about survival of its troops, it has never had the reputation for providing the utmost comfort for them. This chart, however, provides a good starting point. (One interesting point the chart demonstrates is that a person can sleep outdoors in safety, if not perfect comfort, at -60°F with only four inches of insulation. Personally, I balk at that figure; I believe something more like six to eight inches of insulation is necessary for the comfort that enables one to sleep.)

Another source of information about insulation is from Recreational Equipment Inc. The results of its testing appear in an excellent book, *Backpacking: One Step at a Time* by Harvey Manning. Following is a chart showing the test results:

COMFORT RANGES OF GARMENT LAYERS*

Garment	Material	Weight	Thickness	Comfort Range
Thin poly top	Polypropylene	6 oz.	0.07"	+40 to +70°F.
Fleece sweater	Polyester	19 oz.	0.20"	+30 to +60°F.
Pile jacket	Polyester	21 oz.	0.50"	+15 to +50°F.
Poly-fill parka	Quallofil	21 oz.	1.00"	−10 to +30°F.
Gore-Tex shell	Gore-tex	22 oz.	0.09"	+40 to +70°F.

In Combinations	Total Thickness	Comfort Range
Poly top + Gore-Tex shell	0.16"	+25 to +55°F.
Poly top + pile jacket	0.57"	+10 to +40°F.
Poly top + pile jacket + Gore-Tex	0.66"	− 5 to +20°F.
Poly top + poly-fill parka	1.07"	−20 to +25°F.
Poly top + pile jacket + poly-fill parka	1.57"	−40 to +10°F.
Poly top + pile jacket + poly-fill parka + Gore-Tex	1.66"	−50 to −10°F.

* Tests were conducted by the REI Quality Control Department, assuming (1.) an "average" person, not exceptionally thin or stocky or unduly fatigued and with normal metabolism; (2.) a uniform amount of insulation over the entire body; and (3.) dry garments (wet insulation is 9°– to –50°F less warm). These tests, like the Natick tests, *don't account for wind or wetness,* and they assume an equal amount of protection over the entire body.

Since these conditions are not what you will face in the real world, the charts must be used carefully. They are valuable, but their real use should be as a starting point, with the comfort range adjusted downward 20° to 30°F. With enough experience and exposure to the elements, you will begin to be comfortable with your knowledge of clothing combinations and what works to keep you really warm. If you think you have to settle for feeling cold, reread this chapter carefully. **When your heat in equals your heat out, you are at thermal equilibrium and will be comfortable. If your heat out is at a rate faster than your heat in, you are not using enough insulation, assuming you are protected from wind and wet.** It's really that simple.

FACING THE ELEMENTS: TEMPERATURE WIND AND WATER

Temperature, wind and water are the basic elements that cold weather clothing must deal with to protect us effectively. If you ignore any one or more of these elements in a normal situation, you can wind up in an uncomfortable situation. But if you ignore even one element in extraordinary circumstances, such as being without shelter, you set yourself up for extreme discomfort, possibly amputated limbs or even death. Unfortunately, too many people have discovered this when it was too late to make a correction.

Temperature

Temperature is the factor that tells us, without much conscious thought, to increase our clothing. Again, this should point to one of the most important points of this book: THICKNESS = WARMTH. I say *should* because our upbringing prevents it from being obvious. One reason for this is that practical considerations (primarily the need to make a profit) causes clothing manufacturers to make clothing that is comfortable for average temperatures. For example, winter jackets are designed for the average person in an average winter temperature. If the average winter temperature is somewhere around 38°F where you live, it's obviously possible that on any given day the temperature can be lower by another 30 or 40 degrees, or more. If the manufacturer produced clothing thick enough to handle the lower temperatures, most people would be too warm most of the time.

I own a winter parka made with two layers of double-thick polyester batting and a thin nylon shell. When I first bought it, I waited for a windy, zero degree day to try it out. In that cold, I thought I would need a sweater, so I put one on. I walked about a block before I had to unzip the parka. Seven blocks later (about half a mile), I was sweating, even though the coat was open. I love that parka, but I wear it only for winter camping. (It's interesting that two years later the same manufacturer started making that parka with only one layer of polyester batting.) The point is that the normal winter jacket is thinner than it needs to be to handle very cold weather, yet we associate such clothing with winter and therefore with very cold weather. We add a thin sweater under our jacket or coat and don't understand why we are still cold. Our mind set tells us we are wearing a "winter" jacket and so should be warm.

Our assumptions about normal winter clothing keep us from realizing a basic truth: THICKNESS = WARMTH. Another factor that keeps us from seeing this truth is that fashion often dictates what people wear, even while their teeth are chattering. Many people go without a hat in the dead of winter, and most concentrate insulation on their upper torso and never think of adding insulation on their legs. Only in recent years has it become fashionable for women to wear knitted leggings over their slacks or stockings; for their sake, I hope this fashion lasts. Again, the point is that our ordinary winter clothing habits keep us from realizing what otherwise would be obvious. If you wear thicker jackets but still ignore your head and legs, it's easy to lose more heat than your body can produce. So we shiver and never learn the lesson that THICKNESS = WARMTH.

Fashion also keeps many of us from having appropriate thickness in our outerwear because we want to appear thin at all costs, including our comfort. Few people would think of wearing a medium-size jacket with a larger jacket over it for extra warmth, yet a vest and jacket are acceptable. I'm not saying this is what it takes to be warm, but there might be some temperatures at which you might be forced to choose between what works and what is fashionable. As the temperature gets lower, your insulation should get thicker; you should cover enough of your body so that the heat escaping is not greater than the heat it can produce. Exactly how thick your insulation should be for a given temperature is something that requires your experimentation (see pp. 32-33). No two people (and no two basal metabolisms) are exactly alike. If you feel cold, you are cold, and you should add insulation. If you feel warm, you are warm, and you should decrease insulation. This is why the layering principle is so workable for maintaining your comfort level. If you wear three or four half-inch thick garments rather than one two-inch thick jacket, you can easily modify your insulation by wearing as many layers as you need for changing conditions. If you wear only the thick jacket, you will spend most of the time being either too warm or too cold.

Wind

Wind is an important factor affecting your ability to stay warm. Your body heat warms the air inside your clothes, and this then warms a thin layer of air just outside your clothes. In still air, this thin outer layer of warm air is dissipated by natural convection, meaning that the warmer air rises and is displaced by colder air. When the wind blows, it quickly dissipates this warm air; this is called forced convection. If the wind is strong, the warm layer is whipped away as soon as it starts to form; this results in more rapid chilling of first the insulation and then the body.

In arctic regions, when a real gale begins, the natives stop their travel and immediately start to build igloos. There they'll wait out the storm because they consider the wind their enemy; they know full well the danger it creates. Some northern tribes have the ability to sit in a trance-like state, with a lowered pulse rate and slowed breathing, to conserve energy while they wait out a storm that can last for days. Animals in the far north instinctively bury themselves in snow when a hard, windy storm hits. The temperature just under the surface of the snow remains close to the temperature prevailing when the snow first fell. If that temperature was, say, 25°F and the present temperature is -20°F with a strong wind, you can see why the snow can provide lifesaving protection.

Modern man, being used to the protection of civilization, is often unaware of the danger created by strong winds in frigid temperatures, and he tries to bull his way through. This can result in a human statue which others have to find, remove, thaw out and bury. An understanding of, and healthy respect for, the wind is a necessity for outdoor travelers. Some of us are familiar with the wind-chill phenomenon and the charts that express it. Wind-chill is a combination of temperature and wind; charts show the effects of that combination.

WIND-CHILL CHART

Wind (MPH)	Temperature (Degrees F.)										
0	50°	40°	30°	20°	10°	0°	-10°	-20°	-30°	-40°	-50°
10	40°	28°	16°	4°	-9°	-21°	-33°	-46°	-58°	-70°	-83°
20	32°	18°	4°	-9°	-21°	-39°	-53°	-67°	-82°	-96°	-110°
30	28°	13°	-2°	-18°	-33°	-48°	-63°	-79°	-94°	-109°	-125°
40	26°	10°	-64°	-21°	-37°	-53°	-69°	-85°	-100°	-116°	-132°

For example, if we were in a 20-mph wind and the temperature was 20°F, our body would perceive the temperature as –9°F. We can use this knowledge by wearing a windproof outer shell and increasing our insulation (remember: THICKNESS = WARMTH). The wind-chill chart isn't totally realistic in that it is designed to give equivalent temperatures which would be felt on bare skin, thus predicting frostbite danger points. It doesn't provide an accurate equivalent temperature for insulation differences, but still it may be used as a guide. A windproof outer layer will practically negate the effects of the wind if it also stops the "chimney effect" (air traveling from the cuffs and waist up through the neck area). Since a windproof layer won't allow air to penetrate it, cold air can't get in to replace the warmer air inside our clothing. However, it can't prevent the wind from removing the thin layer of warmed air outside the garment.

Examples of windproof clothing are: Any tightly knit nylon fabric (partially windproof); almost any waterproof garment; any microporous fabric, such as the waterproof, breathable laminates (such as *Gore-Tex*).

Many people don't take the wind into account when they dress and don't understand why their otherwise warm wool coat isn't keeping them warm on a cold, *windy* day. Even tightly knit wool material will only slow the passage of the wind, and a loosely knit garment will leak air as a sieve leaks water. When it's about 55°F and breezy, a thick sweater alone just won't cut it, nor will a thin nylon shell jacket. If, however, you put the nylon shell over the sweater, you might be comfortable even at a few degrees lower than 55°F. Something people don't appreciate until they experience it is the windproofing capability of waterproof, breathable laminates (see section on Materials). When I initially wore a *Gore-tex* jacket for skiing, the first thing I noticed was how warm I stayed in high winds. The jacket was much more windproof than the ordinary nylon shell jackets I was accustomed to. I enjoyed the extra warmth, because even on a calm day I was creating my own high winds by skiing down the mountain. Since calm days are the exception in winter, it pays to have a good windproof outer shell.

Water

Few people are aware of how dangerous wetness can be. There are no charts on the effect of moisture in our insulation. Because water is extremely dense compared with air (that is, it has many more molecules in a given volume), it's much easier for a body to conduct heat to water since so many more molecules are in contact at once. Also, water has a higher heat capacity than air; this means it takes more heat to raise a molecule of water one degree than it takes to raise one molecule of air the same degree. A body that is totally immersed in water will lose heat to it more than 240 times faster than in still air. This shows why it's so very important to keep your insulation dry in cold weather.

A common misconception about the relationship between water and cold is that cold, humid air makes you feel colder than cold, dry air. This is opposite to the way things really work. Humid air contains water vapor, which is a gas, and not water as a liquid. Water is a good conductor of heat, but water vapor is almost the same as air, being a poor conductor of heat (or a good insulator). Water vapor is dangerous only when it gets inside your insulation and condenses to become water. Water vapor always has the effect of making the temperature seem a little higher. That's why we dehumidify the air in our homes in the summer and use humidifiers in the winter.

Very cold, very humid air simply doesn't exist. The ability of the air to hold moisture is dependent on temperature. The lower the temperature of the air, the less moisture it can hold. The humidity figure given to us by the weatherman is only the percentage of the total moisture possible for the reported temperature. If the humidity is reported as 60 percent for a temperature of 60°F and later you hear about humidity of 60 percent at 40°F, the moisture in the air is much less in the later report. That's why they call it "relative" humidity; it relates humidity to temperature.

In very cold temperatures, around 20°F and below, low humidity is also a problem because it speeds the loss of moisture from your skin and your lungs, which can cause dehydration. In a cold environment, even a slight amount of dehydration can adversely affect your basic physical ability, especially your ability to maintain warmth. People complain: "That moist air chills you right to the bone" or "That cold humid air goes right through you." These complaints are common when the air is cold *but dry*. Cold, dry air causes rapid evaporation of moisture from your skin, with an attendant loss of heat. Cold, windy air is actually the culprit that's making you feel cold. The antidote is more insulation and a windproof outer shell protecting that insulation.

The essential problem we face in dealing with wetness is that it comes from two directions. We can get drenched from the outside with rain, melting snow or mist; we also can get soaked from the inside via sensible perspiration (sweat) and insensible perspiration (water vapor which keeps the skin moist but also evaporates into clothing and condenses there). To deal effectively with wetness, you must keep both your insulation and yourself dry, protecting yourself from moisture from without and from within. Outside moisture can be dealt with by using a waterproof shell fabric on top of your insulating layers. Inside moisture buildup can be handled in several ways: venting; reducing the rate of physical activity; reducing insulation layers; using a vapor barrier between you and your insulating layers. Venting means using clothing openings at the neck, waist, wrists, legs and front to allow some measure of airflow to carry away moisture-filled air in the insulation. Underarm zippers, sewn into some of the better parkas, are excellent venting devices. Velcro closures on sleeves of the best jackets and parkas allow effective control of the wrist area. Venting works by natural convection (the "chimney effect"). Venting can also be used to prevent overheating to some degree, especially when you can't stop to remove insulation.

Moisture buildup can, and should, be controlled by adapting your activity rate. Since your muscles are only about one-third efficient, they give off a lot of waste heat. If you are comfortably clothed for a given energy output (activity level) and you suddenly increase that output, your muscles will soon cause you to overheat. Your skin then will start to sweat to cool you down. Your body doesn't know how much clothing you have on and will keep sweating into your clothing to try to reduce its overheating. Your mind, however, does know, so a conscious effort is required to slow down, reduce your insulation and/or vent to prevent the body's normal reaction of sweating. A vapor-barrier is anything that prevents the passage of water in its gaseous form. Some waterproof materials are not vapor-barriers, but all vapor-barriers should be waterproof. A vapor-barrier layer between you and your insulation effectively protects your insulation from water vapor. The vapor-barrier is an extremely important factor in this book; it will be discussed in more detail in coming pages.

THE LAYERING PRINCIPLE

The most effective way to maintain warmth and comfort level in varying cold conditions is by using multiple clothing layers rather than just one garment. There are two basic reasons for this. As previously mentioned, you may change the amount of insulation you are wearing by adding or removing various thicknesses of insulating layers. You may choose appropriate materials for each layer to provide the protection you need. For instance, you wouldn't want to wear an ordinary nylon or wool shell to protect you from a heavy rain. Likewise, you wouldn't want to rely on a thin nylon shell for its insulation value. A waterproof, breathable fabric or a coated nylon material can handle both rain and wind, so some layers may do double duty. Subsequent chapters will discuss layered clothing systems.

3
CLOTHING SYSTEMS & MATERIALS

Clothing systems may be categorized in three distinct types. In increasing order of effectiveness they are:

Breathable *(good)*
Waterproof/Breathable *(better)*
Vapor-Barrier *(best)*

THE BREATHABLE SYSTEM

This is the most widely known and used of the three systems. In most situations, it is adequate; in very cold conditions, it is the least protective system; in wet weather, it can be deadly.

The breathable system consists of three basic layers: 1.) a thin underwear, or transport, layer; 2.) middle insulative layers; and 3.) an outer shell fabric. The transport layer, or underwear, keeps the skin dry and therefore warm and comfortable. It does this by being non-absorbent and by wicking moisture away from the skin; the best materials for this purpose are polyester and polypropylene. The best weaves should be fine enough to be comfortable to the skin but not fine enough to allow moisture to build up between the fibers. A net-weave in either of these materials is excellent for underwear. A thin layer of regular-weave polyester or polypropylene on top of a net-weave material makes a particularly warm combination.

The second, or middle, layer is the insulative layer. It may be made up of one or more layers of either the same, or different, insulators. Again, it should be pointed out that **THICKNESS = WARMTH**. Air trapped in small pockets (smaller than ⅛ inch) is the real insulation, not the material that is trapping it. This layer might contain a wool sweater and/or a down vest or jacket, pile fabric jacket, polyester batting jacket or any combination of other insulators. The point is to get this layer thick enough for the conditions you expect and adjustable enough for any variations you might encounter.

The third layer is the outer shell. In the breathable system, this layer serves double duty: 1.) It provides strength to protect the middle insulating layers; and 2.) It protects against the wind by being tightly woven (but not too tight because that would impair the breathability of the system).

The outer shell must protect the insulation from such things as brush, twigs, rocks, sharp ice, etc. You can imagine what would happen to a down jacket if its outside fabric were torn; it would look like the aftereffects of a pillow fight. Some polyester insulations are subject to the same fate. A strong outer shell is a necessity.

THE WATERPROOF/BREATHABLE SYSTEM

This has the same basic three layers as the breathable system except for the last, or shell, layer which has been modified to include one of the new "miracle" membrane fabrics. These fabrics are called a "miracle" because they accomplish what has been sought by explorers, mountaineers and other outdoorsmen for centuries: they breathe and allow water vapor to escape from inside, but are impervious to water from the outside.

The most widely known of these materials (and the first to be developed) is *Gore-tex* fabric, manufactured by the W L Gore Co. This is one of only a few fabrics which starts out as a separate membrane and is bonded to the shell fabric. The others are coated onto the outer fabric. Technically, they all form membranes, or boundaries, which have the desired physical properties. Other brands include *Entrant, Thintec, Helley-tech, and Ultrex:* the list is expanding.

It is now possible for outdoor travelers to be protected from being drenched in an unexpected squall. A climber on the side of a cliff may not be able to don rain gear whenever the weather turns wet; waterproof/breathable fabrics fill the bill here. Skiers now are able to sit in a snow-covered chairlift without getting their behinds soaked and frozen. Runners also are no longer at the mercy of the elements since they can have one garment to protect them from both rain and wind. The windproof quality of waterproof/breathables is much greater than the regular breathable shell fabrics. Those involved in many outdoor activities can benefit from these fabrics. Hiking shoes made with waterproof/breathable fabric liners are a welcome change for hikers. Gloves and mittens have also been improved greatly with the use of these materials. Waterproof/breathable fabric is even being used in some fashionable raincoats.

The Great Letdown

Certain situations may cause breathable systems to cease functioning as intended. Information about such breakdowns is important for anyone who may encounter a cold emergency, and also for those who want to be comfortable while working, traveling or engaging in sports in very cold conditions.

Any time more moisture flows into the insulative layers than can be transmitted through the outermost layer, the system is in the process of breaking down (losing its insulative value). This can happen in many ways. For example, if you are in a cool environment with high humidity and the weather suddenly turns much colder, humidity will be trapped in your insulation and will start to condense. If you increase your energy output without opening your insulation or without removing some insulation, you will start to perspire, and moisture will be trapped in your insulation.

The worst thing about breathable systems is that they break down when you need your insulation most — that is, in very cold conditions. In temperatures below about 15°F (cold that winter outdoorsmen often encounter), when the outer layer of clothing becomes about as cold as the external air, very little moisture will be able to get through this layer. Moisture will condense before it gets close to the outermost layer and freeze as it gets closer to it. This creates an impermeable layer of frost; additional perspiration, as well as most of the moisture not frozen, will wick back to your skin. There it will be re-evaporated by your body heat and be pushed outward only to re-condense when it reaches a point close to the frost. As it condenses, it gives up heat, much of which is lost to the environment. That process now will repeat itself. A real danger is that the timing of this cycle may be from a half hour to an hour, during which you build up heat when you most want to shed it, and then you cool off much too fast when you again want to retain heat. Thus, the possibility of getting hypothermia (subnormal body temperature) in a short time is very real. The colder the weather, the more this cycle works against you. To make up for the loss of insulative capability of clothing systems due to moisture buildup, thicker insulation and good venting are needed. The most effective cure is to get away from breathable systems and use vapor-barrier in very cold conditions.

THE VAPOR BARRIER SYSTEM

A little history is in order here. The vapor barrier idea is relatively new to Western man, but it has been used for thousands of years in the far north by natives such as the Inuit (who regard the name Eskimo as derogatory). The use of vapor barrier was rediscovered in the 1950's by Jack Stephenson, who is also the foremost proponent of its use and its principal supplier for many years. We all owe a debt of gratitude to Stephenson for his work in bringing us the final piece of the puzzle. He has taught us how to put together likely the most effective clothing system ever created, one that handles all four elements: temperature, wind, external moisture *and* internal moisture. This point cannot be taken too lightly. There surely are people living today who still have all their fingers and toes (and maybe their lives) because they used vapor barriers to protect their insulation. Cold weather emergency gear which does not include vapor barrier liners is totally inadequate in light of the present knowledge.

Stephenson should also be recognized for his efforts to break through the mindset of modern society regarding clothing breathability. To show how inflexible our thinking is, consider the use of the so-called "Mickey Mouse" boots during the Korean War. These boots were made of two layers of rubber (or similar material) with wool or foam insulation between. This meant the boot was waterproof from the inside as well as the outside; therefore, no moisture could get to the insulation to destroy its value. The foot soldier didn't have to rely on a change of liner to stay warm, or even on good weather to dry out a wet liner. These thick, warm boots represent the only use of vapor barrier by the US Army to date. Someone in the Army must have known about vapor barrier before deciding to use it in the boot. Since there's clear evidence that it worked well, I'm puzzled about why it never was used for the rest of the body. That's how stuck we are on the breathability idea; we don't see a better solution even when we step in it!

What Is a Vapor Barrier and How Does It Work?

The vapor barrier system consists of four layers. The layer next to the skin is a thin underwear layer of either polyester or polypropylene. In this system, the underwear layer is for comfort only and is not a necessity, although I would not want to go without it.

The next layer, which goes over the underwear (or replaces it) is the vapor barrier. Its purpose is to control insensible perspiration; it also prevents almost all perspiration from entering the insulation. This material is usually some sort of plastic, such as polyethylene or a coated nylon. The material should be totally waterproof and as water-vapor proof as possible. Some vapor barrier shirts come with underarm zippers to allow venting; this is a useful feature.

The insulation layers come next and may be any insulation you choose. Down is safest to use as insulation when it is protected by a vapor barrier.

The shell, or outer, layer may be either one of the membrane fabrics such as *Gore-tex* or a coated nylon. Whatever material is used should be totally waterproof. Using a vapor barrier under the insulating layers without using a waterproof outer shell is like winning half the battle. **Both inner and outer water contamination need to be handled.**

In past years, many people were afraid to try the vapor barrier concept because of the common idea that clothing must be breathable to get rid of body moisture. "If you use a vapor barrier, you'll soak in your own sweat," they'd say. This seems like a logical conclusion unless you examine why the body perspires; then the argument breaks down.

The body gives off moisture for only three reasons. One is a reaction to overheating, which causes the body to create sensible perspiration on the skin, where it evaporates and causes cooling. This reaction worked much better thousands of years ago when men were clothed just in their own skin. Now that we wear clothing, the reaction is not quite as effective, but the body doesn't know this so it perspires anyway to try to cool down. But if we're smart, we don't have to perspire. In a winter activity, when we first start to warm up, we can ventilate excess heat through openings in our clothing, remove a layer or two of insulation, or reduce our physical effort.

Another reason the body gives off moisture is to maintain the moisture level of the skin at approximately 75 to 100 percent and thus protect the skin. A lower level than this is too dry, causing discomfort and cracking of the skin. This is why wind is so damaging to the skin: it dries it out! If you maintain a sufficiently high moisture level at the skin, sensors in the skin will communicate that information to the brain and the sweat glands will shut down. In a vapor barrier environment, the moisture level at the skin remains high, the skin is protected and sweat glands don't have to pump out additional moisture.

The third, and last, reason the body gives off moisture is the sudden fear reaction. This doesn't result in much moisture, isn't likely to last long and might not occur often in a cold environment.

Advantages of Vapor Barrier

Since it reduces insensible perspiration and prevents most perspiration from evaporating or getting into the insulation, it therefore stops most evaporative heat loss. The heat lost by evaporating water from the skin is about 980 BTU/lb. of water. That's a lot of heat to lose, since it's possible to lose more than five pounds of water per day if you use a breathable system. You would lose more than just the heat of evaporation; you also would lose the considerable heat contained in the water before it evaporated.

The vapor barrier blocks moisture, dirt, body oils and salt from getting into and contaminating your insulation. This means that the heat-retention capability of your insulation remains intact throughout the day. Since trapped (or still) air is your real insulation, any molecule of dirt or water which displaces air degrades your insulation. Breathable systems allow this; vapor barrier systems do not. A side benefit is that your clothing stays cleaner, and needs less frequent washing.

Vapor barrier helps prevent dehydration of the body. In winter travel you may lose more than two quarts of water per day through insensible perspiration alone. This is because the cold air is so dry that the body has to pump a lot of moisture to keep the skin from chapping and cracking. Since this is stopped by the vapor barrier, you retain valuable water. Winter campers are urged to drink four to five quarts of water per day to prevent dehydration. This is difficult to do even in the best conditions; most campers wind up at least partially dehydrated. Even a slight amount of dehydration increases your chances of getting frostbite. To a significant degree, vapor barrier helps prevent this.

With vapor barrier, you can regulate your clothing system much more quickly than with a breathable system. The reason for this is that you receive immediate feedback when you start to get too warm. The feedback is the perspiration which starts as soon as your body senses the overheated condition. In a breathable system, this perspiration may be diffusing into, and degrading, the value of your insulation for some time before it is noticed. With vapor barrier, there is no place for the moisture to go, so you notice it immediately and can take action quickly to cool off. It's important to remember that vapor barrier controls insensible perspiration, but you have to control sensible perspiration (sweat) by venting, reducing insulation or slowing down.

Time and energy are saved. Winter campers and climbers carry fuel to melt snow for their water, but with vapor barrier less fuel needs to be carried because less water is needed. No time need be lost drying out wet clothing or sleeping bags in the morning. Actually, this is a great safety feature. Without vapor barrier, if the weather doesn't cooperate by allowing sleeping bags to dry, the situation may become life-threatening in only one or two nights.

The "sin" of sweating is more easily forgiven with the vapor barrier system. Even if you wind up sweating because of carelessness in the control of your clothing and/or energy output, the vapor barrier will prevent moisture from contaminating your insulation. The vicious cycle (perspiration evaporating, condensing, re-evaporating) cannot now get started in your insulation. This safety factor may be a lifesaver. (But if you ignore the perspiration, you can become seriously dehydrated).

The vapor barrier system is the most efficient system possible. Evaporative heat loss is mostly eliminated; the insulation value of the clothing does not decrease from moisture buildup; and less insulation is needed than in a breathable system. If the same amount of insulation were to be carried, the extra layer or layers would be a safety factor against colder weather.

To be as objective as I can about something as positive and workable as this system, I'll try to list the drawbacks I see:

Vapor barrier is for control of insensible perspiration only; it does not prevent perspiration due to overheating, and this must be handled consciously.

Experimentation is needed by anyone using vapor barrier for the first time; because it is more efficient, it is therefore easier for you to overheat until you learn how much insulation you need and how quickly you should ventilate or reduce layers when and if you start to perspire.

Perspiration is less comfortable in the short run since it can build up if you don't handle it. (It's still safer because moisture doesn't get into the insulation);

If I did sweat, I wouldn't want to be around friends when I take off the vapor barrier layer since it can get a little ripe in there; the shower is the best place for that. I don't know if there are any harmful effects of keeping the vapor barrier layer on for more than a few days at a time. However, the skin should be cleansed whenever possible.

To conclude, the vapor barrier system is not only the most efficient clothing system, it is more importantly the *safest* clothing system. Although I've referred mainly to winter campers and climbers in regard to benefits of vapor barrier, its use is adaptable to many outdoor winter activities. My own use of vapor barrier includes alpine skiing, running, hiking and camping. My polyethylene survival suit (vapor barrier shirt and pants) weighs less than seven ounces. I always carry it in my pack, even in summer.

MATERIALS

In the previous section, clothing systems were categorized in three general types: Breathable *(good);* Waterproof/Breathable *(better);* and Vapor Barrier *(best).*

Each of these systems consists of different clothing layers. This section discusses various materials that may be used in the different layers. Three of the basic layers are used in all three systems: an underwear layer, a thermal insulation layer and an outer protective cover. The vapor barrier system adds a waterproof/vaporproof membrane instead of, or over, the underwear layer. The materials will be listed in the approximate order of the best first.

Materials Used In Underwear Layer

Group	Fiber	Absorbency
I Best	1) Polyester	0.5%
	2) Polypropylene	0.3%
	3) Chlorofiber	0.3%
II (2nd Best)	4) Acrylics	1.3 — 2.5%
	5) Silk	5.0%
	6) Nylon	4.5%
	7) Wool	17.0%
III (Worst)	8) Cotton	8.0%
	9) Rayon	11.0%

The list is divided into three groups. I consider the three fibers in the first group to be the best for cold weather undergarments. The important quality all three have in common is that they absorb almost no water. This means that although they can hold some moisture between the fibers, no moisture can get inside the fibers. The more moisture your insulation absorbs, the lower its insulating value. So the first group retains your insulation better by being less affected by water contamination. Since all the materials can hold some moisture between the fibers, the best fibers will be those that can wick moisture away from your skin before it evaporates. The first three fibers here fill the bill, although sometimes the manufacturers use chemical treatments or mechanical reworking of a fiber to achieve the wicking action.

The purpose of the underwear layer is to provide some warmth and, in ordinary clothing systems, to keep moisture away from the skin by transporting it to the next layer by wicking, or capillary, action. The thinner fabrics don't provide much insulation, but they do keep you more comfortable by preventing the chimney effect (removal of the layer of air next to your skin). For more warmth, manufacturers make thicker "expedition weight" underwear. These are even better at stopping the chimney effect.

Polyester is the latest superior fiber used for cold-weather underwear. It absorbs only about 0.5 percent of its weight in water, it can be treated to achieve good wickability, and its maintenance is easy. You can wash and dry polyester by machine, whereas more care is needed with polypropylene, which has a lower melting point and should be air dried. By comparison, cotton absorbs 8 percent of its weight in water, and wool absorbs 17 percent. (Remember, water conducts heat much more quickly than air; so the more water a fabric absorbs, the worse its insulative value.)

The major makers of polyester underwear are DuPont (*Thermax*) and Patagonia (*Capilene*). *Thermax* is a hollow fiber and may be warmer and lighter weight, depending on the weave; it has a convoluted surface which helps it to wick moisture. *Capilene* is treated at the ends of the fibers to increase its wickability; this also makes it softer against the skin and spreads the moisture out on the surface of the material so that it evaporates faster. I consider both to be excellent products.

Polypropylene was the first of the fibers treated for wickability for cold weather, and among campers and climbers, it's still the best known of the winter underwear fibers. It's usually chemically treated for better wickability; this can be partly lost in washing. (It's a good idea to use a fabric softener to restore some of the wickability in polypropylene.) The drawbacks to "polypro" are that it gets a little stiffer with age, it can absorb more body oils than polyester can, and it can be ruined in the drier if you aren't careful. Its good points are that it absorbs only about 0.3 percent of its weight in water, it's thirty percent lighter than wool or polyester, and it's usually less expensive than the other super fibers because there's more competition in the "polypro" market than in the others. In using polypropylene, I've found that it stiffens somewhat with age, yet remains quite comfortable.

Chlorofibre is spun polyvinylchloride. It's absorbency is close to nil, such as polypropylene. It's sold under the name of "Blue-John's" and is marketed by Peter Storm. The Damart company markets what it calls "Thermolactyl"; this, I think, is a combination of spun PVC and acrylic. The primary quality, non-absorbency, puts it in the top three, although it is much more expensive than the others.

The second group of fibers is not as good as the first group for the underwear layer. Most of the fibers in this group have too great a capacity to absorb and hold moisture, which makes them lose insulative value. This also can keep the skin wet and cold. Wool is still spoken of in some quarters as being the best material for underwear. The claims that it retains warmth when wet is great advertising hype but far from the truth. Wool can absorb moisture into its fibers before you notice that it's getting wet. To repeat an important point: **Moisture degrades the insulative value of fabric**. Every molecule of water that replaces air, even in the fibers, will conduct heat away from you more quickly (240 times more quickly!) than the air it displaced. Once the wool gets wet between the fibers as well, you begin to notice dampness **and the cold**. In cold weather, water contamination is to be avoided like the plague.

Wool doesn't wear as well as the synthetics, and it needs more care. As a second choice (if money is a consideration), it isn't a bad material, if you don't allow it to get wet. Some manufacturers promote a two layer system of polypro and wool. They call it hydrophobic/hydrophyllic (water hating/water loving), where the poly keeps moisture away from the skin while the wool layer absorbs it. Two layers of polypropylene or polyester would be much better, even one layer will keep your skin dry and comfortable. You don't want any absorbant material in your insulation system, regardless of its location.

Silk is very comfortable against the skin because it's so soft. It's also rather expensive and absorbs too much moisture, and is therefore not ranked in the top group.

Acrylics are used in some underwear and are not as bad in moisture absorption as some fibers in the second group. Sometimes the acrylics are combined with cotton, which lowers their value as good winter underwear. On the other hand, their cost is usually lower than the products from fibers in the first group; this makes them a good value as long as they are kept dry.

Nylon is sometimes used as an additive fiber for some underwear to increase the strength of the other fibers. It's often found as reinforcement for wool socks to give better wear. It can be made to feel like cotton, so it can be very comfortable as underwear. When used alone as underwear, it's as absorbent as silk; therefore, it's not as desirable as fibers from the first group.

The last group, which consists only of cotton and rayon, I consider to be too absorbent for use as outdoor underwear. Rayon isn't used much for underwear, but cotton is used extensively. The reason is probably the price and the soft feel of cotton. Thermal underwear made from cotton is usually the least expensive, but it's not a great value. Because it absorbs water like a sponge, it's more difficult to dry out than most of the other fibers. When cotton gets wet, it keeps the wearer soaked, completely wetting the micro-environment next to the skin. In addition, as it evaporates from the skin, the rate of heat loss becomes enormous. A thin layer of cotton underwear is usually not dangerous to anyone who knows how to stay dry in rough weather, but to wear other cotton clothing in winter is ill-advised. Or shall we say *deadly*?! The single worst clothing item for cold weather skiing, camping, hiking or climbing is cotton dungarees or jeans.

Materials Used In Insulation Layers

The ideal insulator would weigh next to nothing, be as thin as a tissue, be compressible down to a tiny volume, block the transfer of heat indefinitely, be totally unaffected by moisture, body acids or oils, and cost almost nothing. In the real world, this insulator doesn't exist, so we must choose among the available materials to give us the best of the qualities we need. There are some clear preferences when the qualities of the materials and the desired properties are considered.

The lightest and most compressible insulation has traditionally been waterfowl down. By using synthetics, fiber manufacturers are trying to catch up. Unfortunately, down is dangerous to outdoorsmen when wet, and it's very expensive. The micro-fiber insulations, such as *Thinsulate* and *Thermolite*, are very thin, but are rather heavy, not very compressible and also fairly expensive. Closed-cell foam insulations slow heat transfer better than down or micro-fibers, but they, too, are not compressible. Many of the lightest foams are not suitable for clothing since they are relatively inflexible and have very little strength. The more flexible and stronger foams, such as neoprene, are quite heavy compared to other insulators and are used mostly in water sports. Synthetic fibers come closest to an all around insulator. When manufactured with the right parameters, a synthetic fiber batting can be:

- almost as light as down;
- almost as compressible as down;
- almost as warm as down for an equal thickness;
- non-absorbent;
- non-allergenic;
- about one third to half as expensive as down.

In man-made or natural materials, the way the fibers are spun and the way the insulation is stabilized are as important as the fiber itself. The real insulator, regardless of the material in question, is *air*. All insulators try to trap and block the movement of air to slow the transfer of heat. Since closed-cell foams trap air (or some other gas) permanently in tiny pockets, they are among the best insulators.

SYNTHETIC FIBERS

Today's synthetic fibers are used to make some of the best insulations. Not surprisingly, polyester and polypropylene are in the forefront due to their better qualities and lower price. Compared to the natural fibers we once depended on — kapok, wool, cotton, etc. — the synthetics are far superior. Their primary qualities are, to underscore important points, that they absorb almost no water and they can be produced in whatever denier (thickness) is needed for the fiber.

Two basic types of insulation are made from synthetics. One is a batting (a thick built-up layer of fibers), which must be stabilized by sewing and protected by woven material on both sides; many ski jackets use a batting between the outer and inner shell. The other type is a stand-alone garment which has its fibers connected in such a way they don't come apart. This can be done by weaving the fibers themselves or by intertwining the fibers through a backing cloth. Examples of this are shirts, sweaters, fiberpile fleece and bunting jackets and needle punch (which stands alone but isn't used alone).

To get a single garment thick enough to handle temperatures in the teens requires the use of a batting. The thickest pile jackets are no more than a half-inch thick when new, but a batting garment can be made an inch thick or more. A versatile layered system of cold weather clothing might contain both types of insulation.

FIBER BATTING INSULATIONS:

Polyester battings are made from fibers produced by a number of companies. Following is a partial list:

Dupont: This company has long been in the forefront of fiber research.

Hollofil — A hollow polyester staple (short-fiber). This fiber is not treated with a slick finish and so tends to hold water between fibers more than a treated fiber. Any polyester fiber without a slick finish should not be used where wetness might be a problem.

Hollofil II — A hollow fiber staple with a slick finish which reduces friction between fibers and gives the batting a softer feel. The slick finish is also important because it helps keep fibers from holding water between them.

Quallofil — A four channel hollow fiber with a slick surface. This comes closer than most of the current battings to a downlike feel, drapes well and is used in some arctic sleeping bags and fine jackets.

Thermoloft — This has two types of fibers. One has an inner core for strength and an outer sheath that melt-bonds to the fibers around it to create a strong web of fibers to retain its loft after continued use. The other fiber is a micro-fiber which helps retain more dead air and also blocks radiant heat loss. (Micro-fibers are ultra-thin; they are measured in angstrom units, or millionths of an inch.)

Thermolite — Also contains some melt-bond fibers for strength but has a higher percentage of micro-fibers, so it is warmer for a thinner batt (about 1.7 times warmer than ordinary batting). It's roughly equivalent to 3M's *Thinsulate*, but apparently retains its loft better due to the increased strength from the melt-bond fibers.

3M: This company was the first to use micro-fibers in insulation.

Thinsulate — A thin insulation which is about 1.7 times as warm as an equivalent thickness of ordinary batting. It's best uses are in fashionable jackets, boots, mittens and gloves. It isn't very compressible and since there are so many tiny fibers the advantage is in thinness but not in weight. It's been a blessing for those who want warm hand and foot coverings, as well as for those who worry about their looks in thick insulations.

Thinsulate LDS — This is similar to DuPont's *Thermoloft*; namely, a mid-loft batting which has a mixture of fibers that reflect radiant heat better than the high lofts but is not as dense (or heavy) as the micro-fibers.

Celanese: This company (now part of American Hoescht) was one of the first to help break the habit of using down in outdoor sportswear.

Polarguard — One of the original and still one of the best polyester batts for use in very cold weather gear, such as insulated parkas and serious sleeping bags. *Polarguard* is a long-fiber batt in which the individual fibers are about 100 inches long. The fibers are bonded in production and help support the batting so that it doesn't need as much stabilization (sewing through the batts to keep them from coming apart) as a staple fiber. In theory, a rip in the outer fabric would cause no loss of insulation, whereas with down or a staple fiber, some loss might occur. Celanese also makes a staple fiber called *Loftguard*, which is a hollow fiber similar to Dupont's *Hollofil II.*

American Hoechst: Known for fine *Trevira* polyester, Hoechst's fiber division produces:

Tentron — A staple fiber which has a pentalobal (five-sided) cross section for extra strength.

Nova Loft — A hollow staple fiber with a slick finish. This fiber is close in performance to DuPont's *Hollofil II.*

Pentaloft — A staple fiber also has a five-sided cross section for extra strength and resilience, and it has a permanent slick finish. The cross section of this fiber may be of value in retaining loft over time, and should be checked out by sleeping bag and winter parka manufacturers.

Universe — This is a product to watch as a possible replacement for down. It can be made into batts or blown into pockets like down. It was first released in May 1987.

Eastman Chemical: Makes *KodOfill* which is a staple fiber and *KodOsoff* which is a hollow-fiber staple with a slick finish (similar to DuPont's *Hollofil II*).

Other: Various companies in other countries are in competition for the insulation market. Japan has a micro-fiber insulation called *Eizac*, and Italy has *Thermore* which is a thin insulation.

There are also insulations that use a reflective coating to increase their effectiveness in thinner applications. One of these, *ThermalR* is listed in the foam insulation section. Others are *SP27, L Therm* and *Thermore.*

How the Fibers are Used

When the fibers are formed into thick batts, they are sewn between two outer fabrics for stabilizing. Sleeping bags, comforters, jackets and coats are made this way. The battings can be made up to an inch thick, and more than one layer can be used to make sleeping bags and expedition-weight parkas for extreme conditions. Again, it's thickness that deter-mines warmth (if other things are equal). This rule changes when you introduce the micro-fibers into the insulation. The micro-fibers (*Thermo-lite, Thinsulate, Eizac,* etc.) allow jacket or pants to be about half the usual thickness for an average amount of warmth. They are not used in sleeping bags or thicker expedition-type parkas because they lack the compressi-bility of the high loft batts, and they are too heavy when you make them thick. The large number of tiny fibers that effectively block air movement also trap water between the fibers more efficiently than ordinary polyester batting. This means that if the clothing gets wet, it will be harder to dry than regular batting, so the regular high loft batts have the advantage here.

When the thickness of your insulation is ¾" to 1" that's sufficient to block most of the radiative heat loss by reflecting it off the fibers. The micro-fibers work partly by reflecting radiation better than normal polyes-ter batting, even from a thinner layer, as well as by trapping air better. This means that the micro-fibers are only very efficient in thin battings and lose much of their advantage as they get thicker. This would explain why DuPont produces two different micro-fiber insulations (*Thermolite* and *Thermoloft*), as well as their high loft polyesters, such as *Quallofil.* Each insulation contains the most efficient combination of fibers for the intended thickness (therefore warmth rating) of the clothing.

Pile, Fleece, Bunting

The other type of synthetic insulation, the stand-alone type (such as fiberpile, fleece and bunting), has become important in the last few years. In one or another of its various forms, it first was used by mountaineers and fishermen because it provided more warmth for a given weight than the wool sweaters it replaced. It also was non-absorbent, so that water went between, not inside, the fibers and could be removed in large part by wringing or swinging the garment a few times. (Swinging works better with pile fabrics, which have fibers perpendicular to the fabric, than with fleece or bunting.) This meant that the pile garments were warmer and safer in wet conditions than the old standby, wool. It wasn't long before fashion caught up to function, and now some of these garments are as colorful as can be, and command nifty prices. You can still get decent prices in various catalogue outfits and season-end sales.

The terms pile, fleece and bunting have been used so interchangeably that there is confusion about which is which. In today's terms, **pile** fabrics are those which use a facing cloth, through which the pile fibers are punched or woven. This creates the thickest, and therefore warmest, garment of this group. An example of this type is *Borglite II* pile, which uses a polypropylene outer facing cloth and hollow polyester fibers. This type of garment is for augmenting a thicker insulation in extreme cold or is used by itself under a shell (for wind and water protection) in milder conditions. Since it allows air to pass through it easily, it is used only without a shell in very mild conditions.

Fleece has no separate facing cloth. It is a thickly woven cloth (usually polyester or acrylic) which is brushed to create a fuzzy surface that makes it even thicker and warmer. Early versions of these garments would pill a lot, which didn't bother most outdoor users; it gave the garments a lived in look and also made them a bit warmer because it made them thicker. However, the pilling did bother urban dwellers, so a manufacturer introduced a new type of fleece which is softer and has almost no pilling.

This fabric is produced by Malden Mills and is marketed by various outfits under names such as *Synchilla* (by Patagonia), *Jaegor Fleece* (by Columbia Sportswear) and *Polar Plus* (by Malden). The fabric is not quite as thick as pile, but since it has no separate facing cloth, it may be warmer than pile on a unit-weight basis. Fleece is just slightly better than pile for letting the breezes through, so a shell garment is also appropriate with this fabric.

Bunting used to refer to a fabric more tightly knit than fleece, but today it defines a double-faced fleece. This is one in which both front and back have been brushed to give it more loft.

DOWN

Goose or duck down (plummules from the underbelly, without quills) provides the most warmth for the least weight and also is the most compressible insulation. These qualities have made it a favorite of climbers and campers for a long time. Down usually is blown into pockets in clothing or sleeping bags to keep it from settling and leaving cold spots. Some expedition parkas use two layers of down insulation to provide more thickness and offset the seams to prevent cold spots. Some of the warmest sleeping bags in the world are made with down insulation.

Down is not without some drawbacks. It is the most expensive insulation, and it can easily get wet. When it is soaked, its insulative value is close to nil. This can turn an ordinary outing into a survival struggle. Once down gets soaked, it is very difficult to dry. A good way to reduce the danger of getting a down garment wet is to use vapor barrier between the wearer and the down and also employ a waterproof outer shell. In spite of its drawbacks, down is still one of the best insulations.

WOOL

Wool had been a standard of insulation for many years. Along with kapok, it was used in comforters and sleeping bags in past years. Wool has been used in every layer of clothing and, as noted previously, has a false reputation for retaining its warmth even when wet. While this is not true, many people have been fooled by the hype. The truth is that any wet fabric will cause heat loss faster than any dry fabric. Unfortunately, there are many current, as well as antiquated, source books which still recommend wool as the premier outdoor fiber.

Wool tears relatively easily and doesn't wear especially well, but it may be used in many types of attractive garments. The best place for wool is in the city or ski resorts. Wool makes great looking sweaters and shirts, as well as fashionable outer coats, scarves and other clothing items. It also is good for socks because of its cushioning effect.

Some people rely on heavy wool overcoats to keep them warm in the winter. This is fine until the temperature dips to 10°F or lower, or until a strong wind blows. The weight of wool somehow gives us a sense of security, but that's a false sense. Wool isn't thick enough to retain your warmth below the teens and a strong wind will pass through it and further rob you of warmth. In very cold weather, a tightly woven nylon outer cloth or one of the waterproof/breathables is necessary to protect against the wind, and an insulation thicker than woven wool is needed to retain the body's warmth.

FUR

Fur is an excellent insulator. That's due to its high loft. Fur's main drawbacks are its high price, its weight and the ever-increasing list of endangered species. Modern materials surpass fur in warmth-per-unit-weight because the leather holding the fur is very heavy. It is not suited to outdoor sports because it is incompressible. The primary reason for buying fur is not warmth but fashion, and good imitation fur will look as nice and be as warm as real fur if it's of equal thickness.

FOAMS

Foams are important insulators both for outdoorsmen and urbanites. Foam insulation is used in gloves, mittens, shoes, boots, wet suits, face masks, life vests, jackets, insulated pants, ski suits and sleeping pads. To give an example of just how good foam insulations can be, consider trying to sit on frozen ground when the air temperature is –50°F (assuming you are dressed to be outside in that temperature!). A one-inch thick pad of lightweight closed-cell foam would allow you to sit in perfect comfort. As previously noted, a thin Styrofoam cup that protects your hand from boiling-hot water (212°F) is an even more graphic example of foam slowing heat transfer. Obviously, closed-cell foams are among the best insulations!

Foams used for personal insulation are generally classified as open-cell or closed-cell. Open-cell foam is good when breathability is important, and it usually is less stiff than the closed-cell variety. Closed-cell foam is waterproof and is great for sleeping bag pads, scuba divers' wet suits and any situation in which water infiltration could be a problem. Neoprene is one of the widely used closed-cell foams. It is used mainly for wet suits and insulated waders and more recently for face masks. It is very pliable and strong for a closed-cell foam. Its main drawback is that it also is heavy.

Ensolite (PVC) by Uniroyal was one of the most widely used foams for sleeping bag pads, but it has been replaced by PE (polyethylene) such as Dow's Ethafoam and by EVA (ethyl vinyl acetate) such as Evazote. Both EVA and PE are lighter than Ensolite, and they are unaffected by the cold down to about –100°F. EVA has a slight edge over PE in strength and resistance to ultraviolet rays. EVA is being used more in shoes and boots, due to its strength, shock absorbing ability and warmth. Some companies (such as Rockport) are beginning to make dress shoes with thick EVA soles, which should be great in winter.

Open-cell foams are also used as insulation. Some people prefer thick (1½-inch) open-cell foam to the thinner closed-cell foams for sleeping pads. The thicker open-cell foams are softer and provide more cushion against the hard ground. The extra thickness is valulable not only for cushioning but also for warmth, because closed-cell foams are more thermally efficient. The open-cell foams also pose more risk in wet conditions. One company (*Thermarest*) uses a waterproof cover and a sealable valve to create an inflatable open-cell foam sleeping pad. This combines the best virtues of an air mattress and an open-cell foam pad; it's comfortable, warm, compressible and waterproof. This type of pad is not as effective in extreme cold because it doesn't expand as much as you would like for comfort. And, if you breathe into it to help it along, the moisture from your breath will freeze inside the pad. A pad of this type is more suitable for 20°F and higher. An ordinary air mattress allows too much heat loss by convective air currents to be effective in cold weather. (The exception to this is a down-filled air mattress.)

Efforts were made in recent years to use thick open-cell foam as clothing insulation in jackets, but they did not sell well; bulkiness and poor draping qualities may have been the cause. This foam was used more successfully in mittens and gloves. Modern efforts at using foam for clothing are aimed at making the insulation thinner. One of the more radical new insulations is called *Thermal/R*.

Thermal/R: This insulation, from a company of the same name, is a thin, three-layer laminate which addresses several sources of heat loss. The first layer is a clear polyolefin which is dimpled to increase its thickness and has small holes in the dimples for ventilation. The middle layer is open-cell foam, which is better than a fiber insulation at slowing convective currents. The outer layer is also dimpled polyolefin, but this layer has a reflective coating applied to it. The reflective coating serves two purposes: it reflects much of the radiative energy back to the wearer, and its outer side has very low emissivity, which means it is a poor radiator and thus slows radiative heat loss to the outside. The inner and outer layers of polyolefin have small ventilation holes which don't allow as rapid a transfer of air as normal fabrics. This makes the material more windproof.

Since this composite material addresses convective, radiative and evaporative heat loss, it might be expected to outdo an equivalent thickness of ordinary insulation (which handles mostly convection and conduction of air), and indeed this is the case. A more extraordinary claim made for *Thermal/R* is that it is warmer than the micro-fiber insulations (it's ten times thinner than *Thinsulate*). The claimed R-value for 1/32-inch of *Thermal/R* is about R2, which is roughly equivalent to 2/3-inch of ordinary fiber insulation. This should make it popular with ski wear manufacturers due to the fashion advantage of such a thin insulation. It is currently being used in jackets, hats, gloves and shoes. As with other thin insulations, two plus two doesn't quite equal four in the case of *Thermal/R*. The R-value was obtained by handling three sources of heat loss; any additional benefit must be obtained by adding thickness to handle (mostly) air conduction. Beyond a certain temperature (which will vary from individual to individual), you still have to add thickness to get more warmth. I don't mean to detract from the value of *Thermal/R*. It alone won't get you to the top of Mount Everest, but it should be good enough for most fall, and some winter, temperatures in many areas.

Closed-cell foams are the best possible insulation for any activity involving water; scuba diving, kayaking, canoeing, sailing, surfing, boating, water skiing, spelunking, etc. Closed-cell foam is a viable insulation which is immune to water penetration and therefore can't lose its insulative value to wetness.

Spelunkers (cave explorers) are often in areas where underground water makes the going soggy. Since the temperature in many caves stays in the 50s, soaked clothing can be extremely uncomfortable and sometimes deadly. Even with no wind and with temperatures above 50°F, some spelunkers have died from hypothermia underground. Wet clothing plus high heat loss from conduction to the ground are the usual causes. To improve safety for spelunkers, closed-cell foam in their insulation system is needed, as well as a small, thick closed-cell foam pad to sit on when they stop.

Climbers in cold conditions may also benefit from closed-cell foam. Their activity often involves brief spurts of high energy followed by periods of relative inactivity. The highly active periods involve high heat production with its attendant perspiration production. When the climber stops to rest, his perspiration-soaked insulation will cause him to cool down far more than is desirable or safe. This is a threat which cannot be overstated. Excess cooling-down is an additional energy drain that the climber can ill afford. The use here of closed-cell foam (or vapor barrier) would be appropriate. Venting zippers may be placed where the climber may easily adjust them, and when he stops and zips up, his insulation will do its job of keeping him warm instead of soaking up perspiration and causing him to freeze.

MATERIALS USED IN THE OUTER SHELL

The outer shell may be merely the fabric that covers the insulation of a jacket, or it may be a separate piece of clothing. In the most versatile clothing systems, it usually is a separate garment. The shell may be loosely knit and allow air to penetrate; it may be wind-resistant, which slows air penetration, or it may be totally windproof, allowing no air penetration. It may leak water like a sieve, be water-repellent or completely waterproof. It may even allow water vapor to pass through while still being waterproof. It all depends on the fiber, the weave and any chemical treatments and membranes.

Many of the familiar fibers, both natural and synthetic, are used in the outer shells of jackets, parkas, pants, gloves, hats, etc. Nylon comes on strong as one of the best fibers for the outer layer, or outer shell. For the most demanding uses, such as mountaineering and winter camping, where extremely high winds or abrasion to the clothing is a danger, the stronger nylons are a must. Sometimes the strongest nylons are too heavy for an entire shell and are only used as patches in high contact areas such as shoulders, elbows, knees and seat.

The higher the denier (thickness of fiber), the stronger the fabric. Some of the higher strength nylons from DuPont are Ballistics Cloth, *Cordura*, Oxford Nylon and Taslan. From Allied Fibers, the *Caprolan* nylon in the higher deniers is also quite strong. Air-blowing the nylon to produce a rough textured finish (taslanized) is used by various companies; such fabric is useful for skiing and winter mountaineering since it can slow a slide on the snow.

Cordura (also rough-textured) is used in some excellent quality shell garments by some of the leading outdoor clothing manufacturers. It comes in 1000, 500 and 330 denier, all of which are quite strong. It will give you an idea of the strength and abrasion resistance of this material if you know it was used to patch the bottoms of mukluks on the Steger Expedition to the North Pole in 1986. In only one day, the rough arctic ice tore up some of the original moosehide bottoms from the mukluks. The *Cordura* replacements lasted for the next thousand miles — quite a successful field test!

When you don't need the highest strength or abrasion resistance, there are many lighter fabrics which are sufficiently strong for most purposes. Some of the newest fabrics are the high-filament count-nylons which have the strength of the thicker nylons but aren't as stiff, so they drape well and look better in jackets and parkas. The texture of the cloth may be rough, cottony or silky with equally good draping qualities. Some of these new materials are nylons that feel as soft as cotton, such as: *Supplex* from DuPont, *Capima* from Allied Fibers and *Tactel* by ICI. A similar but rougher textured material is *Berguntal* cloth from Columbia Sportswear, which feels like taslan but drapes much better. Previously there were many nylons that felt silky, but the newer ones (such as *Captiva* from Allied) are stronger. Most of the new high-filament nylons are stronger, softer, more windproof and more water resistant. When you take a very high filament count and make it a super-tight weave, you can create a windproof, relatively waterproof cloth that can compete in some instances with waterproof/breathables such as *Gore-tex*. This has been done with a super fine weave polyester from Burlington Industries called *Versatech* and one from Japan called *Super-Microft*. These materials should do well for ski wear and running suits.

WATERPROOF/BREATHABLE FABRICS

When total weather protection is desired, a completely windproof, waterproof outer shell is required. Luckily, any waterproof shell will also be windproof as long as the front zipper closure is well sealed. There are two basic types of waterproof garments: breathable and non-breathable. The breathable types have been on the market only for the past dozen years or so. The earliest versions were a disappointment; they leaked if they got any dirt or body oils on them, or if the seams weren't sealed by the owner. The newer ones are better, but you still have to be careful when shopping. Manufacturers started to seal the seams with tape, but not all manufacturers sealed all seams. To assure the consumer that a garment is completely waterproof, the W L Gore Company (which produced the first breathable/waterproofs) started to label the performance of seam-sealed *Gore-tex* shells, calling them "Rainwear Without Compromise"; this means that any garment so labeled can withstand the equivalent of a three-inch-per-hour downpour (that is one heavy rain!) for a minimum of thirty minutes. For all other garments for which waterproofing is claimed, you have to jump in the shower yourself to verify just how waterproof they are, or perhaps learn where you have to add seam sealant. One or two seams which are not waterproof may not appear to be of much concern, yet in a steady downpour they could wick enough moisture to thoroughly soak your insulation.

There are now three ways of making a shell both waterproof and breathable. One is to laminate a fabric with a membrane that has pores just the right size to permit single molecules of water vapor to pass through but small enough to block larger multiple molecules of water. This is the idea behind *Gore-tex;* PTFE material (the same material that *Teflon* is made from) was stretched to create the pore-size needed. A second way to create a waterproof/breathable garment is to coat a fabric with a polymer material of just the right thickness to give it the appropriate pore-size; some coated materials claim to have no pores at all but pass water vapor molecules between the molecules of the coating. The third method is the extremely tight weave already mentioned. This method is not quite as waterproof as the first two, so for better waterproof quality, the Burlington Company adds a coating to the tight weave in making a material called *Ultrex.*

Some of the other waterproof/breathables are *Helly-Tech, Entrant* (Japan), *Permia* by Somitex, *Waterguard* by Kombi, *Stan-air-lery* (Belgium), *ThinTech* by 3M, *Porelle* and *Helsapor.* There are others, but read the labels carefully. Some are highly water-resistant but not waterproof.

The newest creations in the waterproof/breathable market are: stretch versions; free-hanging lining between the outer fabric and the insulation, allowing use of a completely waterproof liner with fewer seams to seal; fabric which has the waterproof layer attached to the insulation under the outer shell (but not to the outer shell itself); this makes possible much easier waterproofing of the seams and better draping qualities for the outer fabric.

Although a membrane in the outer shell may stop water from entering the insulation, the material of the outer shell which protects that membrane may get very wet. It is desireable to prevent the wetting of the outer shell fibers so that no evaporative heat loss ensues. This may seem like overkill, but every little bit helps. There are two ways manufacturers accomplish this prevention. One is to use a super tight weave fabric such as *VersaTech* or *Super Microft*; the other is to use a water-repellent coating on the outer fabric. Some of the better water repellants are *ZEPEL, Stormshed, HydroGuard* and *Durepel*. That last product is a water and stain repellent which Burlington Industries claims will last indefinitely.

Where breathability is not needed, or where heavy-duty, totally waterproof fabrics are needed for rainwear, a heavier polymer or PVC coating is used. These are used extensively around salt water since the breathable coatings and membranes are affected by salt. Some of the best waterproof non-breathable garments are produced by Patagonia (Seal Coat), Peter Storm, Henri-Lloyd, and Stearns.

ARTICLES OF CLOTHING

Following are some examples of the many and varied types of garments available for the different parts of the body and for different conditions.

Head

Wool (or Orlon) Cap: Good general purpose head cover for cold, but cannot protect well against wind or rain. Some are now sold with *Gore-tex* or similar lining, which improves the cap tremendously.

Balaclava: A thick wool cap that may be worn just as a cap or pulled down over the face and neck because it has cutouts for the eyes, nose and mouth.

Insulated Caps: Can be found with nylon or nylon/*Gore-tex* outer layer and insulated with pile, fleece or micro-fibers (*Thermolite, Thinsulate,* etc.). They usually have a brim which provides a little extra protection from sun and rain.

Crusher: A wool hat with a brim that is thin enough to be crushed into a ball and stuffed in a pocket or pack. It pops back into shape (almost) for wearing. It's good for three-season wear, but not for very cold weather.

Sou'wester: A brimmed rainhat with longer brim in back to keep rain from going down the neck and back (a favorite of fishermen).

Dress hats: Wool, blocked hats provide some protection in cold conditions, but are sorely lacking in very cold weather. Northern Europeans have the right idea; they wear fur hats, which are much warmer because they are much thicker. The larger ones that cover the ears are the best.

The warmest covering for the head is the insulated parka-hood. It should be attached to the parka to provide continuous protection for the head, neck and body. The thicker the insulation in the hood, the warmer it will be. For greatest warmth, the outer shell should be one of the waterproof/breathables to provide rain and wind protection.

Face

Face mask: For extreme cold, this is usually a necessity. There are different types, including masks made of leather, wool, *Gore-tex*/nylon, plastic and foam. I find the neoprene-foam variety very comfortable and warm.

Wool cap/face mask combination: This is what bank robbers use, but not to stay warm. It isn't as comfortable as the balaclava, which leaves slightly larger openings for the eyes, nose and mouth.

Snorkle hood: This is a tunnel-shaped extension of the parka-hood. It helps maintain some relatively warm dead air space in front of your face. This air pocket can't be completely dislodged by the wind all at once, so it keeps your face warmer. To be really effective, the tunnel part should be at least six inches long and not too wide.

Scarves: Excellent for city wear; they may be pulled up or wrapped around the face and neck for protection. Obviously a thick wool scarf will be warmer than a thin silk one because it's thicker and not because of the kind of material.

Neck

Turtleneck: Having a turtleneck on a sweater or on thermal underwear provides good protection for neck area. Polypropylene turtlenecks with zippers for adjustability are great for winter sports.

Neck Gaiters: These are turtlenecks without any shirt attached to them. They are easier to remove than one with the shirt; some are long enough to unroll and protect the lower part of the face.

Scarves: As mentioned above, they are very useful in the city. They should be used with extreme caution in the outdoors and not at all for most sports. If they get caught in machinery, a bad time may be had by all.

High Collars or Hoods: On ski jackets high collars protect the neck very well, since they go past the chin line. Obviously a hooded jacket will protect the neck as mentioned above.

Trunk

Undershirt and regular shirt are the standard first layers for the upper body. Combo shirt/jackets made of wool or polyester fleece are also popular.

Vapor barrier shirts provide protection against insensible perspiration, as well as preventing perspiration from contaminating the insulating layers.

Sweaters: Fleece or pile sweaters are the *in* thing. They're lighter than wool and don't absorb much moisture. The standard wool or acrylic sweaters are still very useful; they conform somewhat to your body shape and therefore help prevent the "chimney effect" of cooler air replacing the layer of warm air next to your body.

Vest: A thick vest of pile, polyester batting or down insulation may be used to add warmth to a clothing system. This is usually easier than combining insulated jackets since the sleeves are sometimes too confining.

Jacket: Many styles are available. A high collar is useful, as are multiple pockets. Some come with double-pull zipper for venting and a storm flap to protect the front closure area.

Parka: This garment was developed over the years as climbers and hikers added more features to gain greater protection from the elements. The parka has a hood (sewn on or detachable), is usually longer than a jacket, may or may not be insulated (if not, it's called a shell-parka) and usually has a double front closure in case of failure of the main zipper. It should have a storm flap over the front zipper; it usually has many pockets, including large "handwarmer pockets" in front. The best parkas have what's called a snow or wind dam (or a snow skirt) at the waist inside to prevent snow or wind from being blown up into the garment. If this feature isn't used, then a drawstring at the waist is usually substituted. The hood should also have a drawstring for adjusting the opening. Some parkas provide two drawstrings in the hood so that it moves with your head (beats looking at something with one eye while your other eye is looking inside your hood). Today's better parkas are usually made from one of the waterproof, breathable materials and may be very colorful. Vents are another high end feature and may be very useful. As is usually the case, the more features, the more expensive. Make sure your parka is strong (not too thin) and not just attractive. Also be sure it fits over the combination of insulating layers you want to wear.

Anorak: This is similar to a shell-parka except the front zipper goes only about 6 inches below the neck, so little wind or rain can go through a front opening. Since modern parkas have efficient double closures in front, the anorak is rather dated. It does have the advantage of being lighter since it doesn't have the full zipper.

Cagoule: A very long anorak (usually waterproof) used by climbers and hikers. Its length enables it to be used as a bivouac sack by the wearer who draws his knees up into the garment.

Poncho: An open-sided, usually waterproof garment with an opening for the head (with a hood). It's long enough to provide some protection for the legs. A poncho is great if there's nothing stronger than a light breeze. Under some conditions (such as strong wind with cold rain), a poncho can get you killed. Unless you're very close to civilization, I would consider a poncho too dangerous for the first twelve months of the year. A rain parka and rain pants are a safer bet.

Hands

Gloves: May be made of many materials. Foams and micro-fibers (such as *Thermolite*) are excellent insulation for gloves. The thicker they are, the warmer. The outer shell should be windproof and preferably waterproof. Wool gloves will not stop the wind but are nice in mild cold conditions. They too, should be thick for warmth.

Mittens: With equal thickness and materials, mittens always are warmer than gloves. Mittens come in many materials.

Specialty gloves are available which allow either one or all fingers to be exposed. This allows photographers, surveyors, hunters, etc., to do work which requires more manual dexterity than is possible when the fingers are covered. Another special glove made of neoprene is for people who work in wet environments or for anyone wanting a combination of vapor barrier and convective/conductive insulator.

Legs

Pants are available in many styles and materials. For warmth, the weight doesn't matter, just the thickness. Also, fuzzy materials are warmer than smooth ones because of their ability to capture more dead air.

Underwear is useful for the legs as well as the trunk in cold conditions.

Warmup pants are available which are lighter and warmer than ordinary pants. They are similar in materials and thickness to expedition-weight underwear except warmups are cut fuller for more freedom of movement.

Insulated pants with nylon outer shells are available in various thicknesses for different degrees of protection. Skiers are the major users of this garment, but it is also used for many other winter activities.

Windbreaker or shell pants are used by hikers, skiers, runners and others. Sometimes these are made of thin nylon and cut loosely to cover warmups, and sometimes they are of very strong, waterproof and windproof material to match the outer shell used for the trunk. The latter type is good in extreme weather conditions.

Feet

Socks are the first line of defense for the feet. In many activities it's common to use two pair of socks so that different materials may be combined to provide different properties. For instance, you may wear a thin inner sock of polypropylene (to help wick moisture away from your foot) and combine it with a thick wool sock (to absorb the moisture, cushion the foot and provide more insulation).

Shoes and boots are available for almost any activity you might imagine. Specialty catalogues are valuable for checking out footwear for your chosen activity. For extra warmth, thickness still counts. Some shoes and boots are available with *Gore-tex* liners for protection against water; some winter boots use *Thinsulate* or *Thermolite* insulation for warmth, while some use superwarm closed-cell foams.

Gaiters are excellent for increasing warmth in this body area that's difficult to keep warm. Gaiters are boot covers that go over the top of the boot and part of the lower leg. They protect against snow getting into boots, and when gaiters are insulated, they provide much more warmth than boots alone.

4
DRESSING FOR WARMTH

This chapter presents examples of clothing combinations that will keep you warm in various activities. Being warm allows you to concentrate on, and enjoy, whatever you're doing; you're unlikely to experience the thrill of skiing, for example, if your feet are freezing. There are many ways to dress for most activities; the following clothing combinations are only suggestions. They are not necessarily the *best* combinations and certainly not the *only* ones or the *right* ones. They are just possibilities for you to consider.

No additional sources of heat, such as fire, batteries, hand warmers or other artificial devices will be considered here. The only heat source you should count on is your own body, fueled by the food you eat. This is not to say that artificial heat sources aren't useful and convenient in some instances, but they are not necessary and should not be relied on.

A key variable in determining how to dress to be warm is the amount of energy our body is generating; this will be affected significantly by our chosen activity. I have arbitrarily grouped activities, based on energy output, into three categories: sedentary, fairly active and very active. Some outdoor activities are easy to put in one category or another, but some resist any pigeonholing. For example, a skier may be very active blasting down a mogul-studded hill or careening down a slalom course, and only a minute later he'll be sitting still in a cold chairlift. Most of the time, however, the average skier is only fairly active; therefore, I labeled skiing accordingly.

These labels are not to be taken as authoritative or inflexible; only *you* know your energy output level in specific activities. In reading about different ways to dress for different activities, don't get hung up on the categories; make any adjustments that suit you. Usually the only change you'll need to make is in the amount of insulation, if your energy output is higher or lower than the given category. Insulation thickness is a variable you determine; your choice can be based on the guidelines and then adjusted to fit your particular circumstance.

Secrets of Warmth

It's appropriate to repeat a few basic ideas for football fans:

It's much easier to stay warm than to try to warm up after getting cold. You must have sufficient insulation for the temperature and wind conditions you encounter, or you'll wind up shivering, stomping your feet, downing hot drinks and doing whatever you can to warm up; all of this will significantly interfere with your being able to enjoy the game.

It takes much more insulation to stay warm when you're sitting still than when you're active. Even if you're excited by the game, you won't be able to generate much heat beyond your basic metabolic level (unless, of course, you do isometric exercises, which would be a little ridiculous when you're in a crowd trying to watch a game.) Notice that the football players put on large parkas and gloves when they go to the sidelines on cold days. They can't afford to let their hands or legs get cold. Even the large amount of energy they expend on the field can't keep them warm for more than a few minutes after they stop. Anyone sitting still needs a lot more insulation than the players on the sidelines who are exercising vigorously every few minutes.

You lose heat faster to a cold solid object (conduction) than to cold air (convection). Therefore, you should take extra measures to retain the warmth in your feet and your seat.

WHAT TO WEAR FOR OUTDOOR GAMES

This depends on the weather. It's smart to be prepared for 10 degrees lower than you expect; then you won't be disappointed if the weather forecast was a few degrees off. *What* you wear isn't as important as *how much* you wear. If you're wearing, say, two thick ski jackets which are equal in thickness to the fur coat of the person sitting next to you, or to another person's down coat, then each of you has about the same amount of heat retention in your insulation. I'll say it again: It's the *thickness* that counts, not the material. (The only limited exceptions to this rule are the micro-fibers such as *Thermolite* and *Thinsulate* and foams such as *Thermal/R.*)

Now we should consider what thickness you'll need for the expected temperature. This is a matter of trial and error for each of us, because so many variables are involved for different people and even for the same person at different times. The Army's *Quartermaster Guide* is a place to start. Since its figures are not conservative, use the insulation thickness specified for sleeping; you can consider that adequate for sitting still:

EFFECTIVE TEMPERATURE INSULATION

(degrees F.)	(inches)
+40	1.5
+20	2.0
0	2.5
–20	3.0

Remember that this chart is just a guide. It doesn't take wind into account, so you have to know what the effective temperature will be *with* wind. It also assumes an even thickness of insulation over the entire body. So if your jacket is thick but your pants are thin, don't expect the listed thickness to keep you warm. If you want to be warm in very cold conditions, you have to insulate all around. The chart is also for an "average man"; if you're a large person you may need less, and if you're thin you may need more.

For example, if you expect 0°F at a football game (including the wind-chill factor), you might bundle up with a few sweaters, a ski jacket and a parka on top. You still might not have the 2½ inches you want, so take along a thick blanket. If this seems like too much, try it anyway. You'd be surprised how hard it is to *overdress* for zero degrees when you're sitting still. If you're wearing too much, you always can take off something and put it behind you. If you bring too little insulation to the game, you'll find it infinitely more difficult to put on a jacket you left in your house. With a little experimenting, you can become proficient at judging just what you will need to stay warm. If you're concerned about looking silly, just pile on most of it after you get to the stadium and put a blanket over it all. Many people wear blankets at a stadium, so you won't feel out of place. What many people don't know is that they can be *really* warm if they wear enough under their blanket.

Face

To protect your face in cold weather, try a greasy skin cream, which seals your pores and prevents evaporation of moisture from your face. Such evaporation would increase cooling, cause chapped skin, and hasten the onset of frostbite. For very cold conditions, say below 10° or 20°F, try a ski mask. You may think you look funny, but people without a mask often long silently for one. The snorkle hood on a parka also protects the face; it sticks out about six inches from your face and maintains in front of you a column of air which the wind can't quickly dissipate, thus retaining some warmth for your face.

Hands

Make sure your hand-covering is thick enough. A pair of thin knit gloves or even thin leather gloves just won't cut it. You need thick gloves or mittens (mittens are warmer than gloves) to stay warm. Even then, if you're sitting still, you may have to keep them under your coat or blanket.

Legs

Many people bundle up enough on top to get by, but they don't bother to wear anything extra on their legs or their feet. These people will be cold. For temperatures under 10°F, you should wear insulated underwear or insulated overpants (such as ski pants) that have zippers all the way down the legs for ease in fitting over your pants and shoes. If you do this, you have a good chance of keeping your legs warm when those around you are shivering. A quilted blanket will also do the trick if it's big enough and can be wrapped around your legs. The combination of both insulated pants and quilted blanket will allow you to handle serious cold, even a bit below zero.

Feet

Try an extra large pair of shoes and wear an extra pair of socks. The shoes should not be tight, or the extra socks will not do any good. Tight shoes cut off your circulation and cause your feet to become painfully cold. Wear shoes with the thickest soles, preferably foam soles. You want as much insulation as possible between you and the cold stadium. If you have an extra piece of foam insulation lying around, cut a 14″ square piece of it to use as a footrest. The difference this makes will surprise you. The thicker the foam, the better. If you can't find foam, use layers of dry newspapers or magazines. If you want to go from 10° to below zero, wear "Moon Boots" such as those skiers use as after-ski boots. They are made of thick foam covered with nylon or other outer material; the foam is super warm and available up to an inch thick.

Seat

If your *gluteus maximus* is in direct contact with a cold seat (and at zero or near it, a seat in a stadium is *very cold*), you are going to be giving up a lot of heat to it. You will be very aware of the discomfort. What you need is good padding between you and the seat. Another piece of closed-cell foam would come in handy. Soft foam is better than hard foam for this purpose, but hard foam is better than a cold seat. Again, if foam isn't available, use a thick layer of newspapers. A wool or polyester blanket, folded to a thickness of about 2 inches, also will keep the fanny warm.

DRESSING FOR MODERATE ACTIVITIES

Downhill skiers have to contend with wide variations in temperature and energy-output. Also, they are almost always in a headwind. Even on a totally calm day, a person skiing downhill at 15 mph has the same conditions as a person standing still in a 15 mph wind. Whether you are rushing past the wind or it is rushing past you, the result is the same: forced convective heat loss. Even when the skier is sitting quietly in the chairlift, he or she is often subject to fierce, cold winds.

The skier must also deal with moisture. If a skier takes a spill, he or she can get a lot of snow into his/her clothing. Sitting in a snow-covered chairlift can give the snow plenty of time to melt in the seat of your pants. Skiing while snow is falling can cause snow to stick to clothing, and this can melt into clothing that isn't waterproof. Skiing in the rain is an obvious way to get waterlogged, if the skier isn't protected by waterproof outer clothing. (Snow is very absorbent and can soak up a few hours of rainfall before it gets mushy; so even if starts raining, quite a few skiers will continue skiing for a while.)

It should be it obvious that the skier should wear a windproof, waterproof (breathable) outer shell over his/her clothing system; this layer can be either part of the ski parka and pants or a separate shell system. Most skiers get away without windproof, waterproof outer shells, but to ensure real warmth it's best to use these materials.

Most skiers handle the problem of insulation thickness (how much to wear) by averaging what they need to stay warm while skiing and what they need for warmth while standing still or sitting in a chairlift. This common "wisdom" runs through the ski world; the "logic" is that if you wear enough to stay warm in the chairlift, you'll sweat too much while skiing and then freeze in the chairlift. I disagree with this reasoning, which holds true only for mogul bashers on average temperature days. For most skiers, the results of this fallacious reasoning are: 1.) Thousands of skiers enduring needless discomfort (freezing in the chairlift anyway); 2.) Short lift lines when the temperature nears zero; 3.) Skiers packing the lodge to warm up with hot drinks; and 4.) Many skiers running short of energy sooner than necessary because they did not stay warm enough during the day. This last point has important implications. Many ski injuries occur late in the day when skiers are tired and their reaction times are slowed. When you stay warm throughout the day, you're conserving energy. This delays the onset of fatigue and translates into more energy in reserve late in the day. When you're not tired, you enjoy skiing more and can ski without the danger that accompanies fatigue.

My preference in ski clothing is to dress for the worst weather I expect to encounter, both while actively skiing and while sitting still in a chairlift for up to half an hour. The way to handle my body's energy output differences (and therefore the differences in insulation needs) is to reduce the effective insulation I'm wearing by venting. Many ski parkas have double pull zippers, and for good reason: they allow you to open your parka as much as you want from either top or bottom. If you open your parka about a third of the way from the bottom and just a little on top, you decrease the effective value of the parka dramatically without having it flap around. Ski warmup pants can also be vented this way if they have a continuous zipper on the legs. If your parka has Velcro adjustments on the cuffs, they also can be opened to allow air to cool you if necessary. A zippered turtleneck is another example of clothing that can be adjusted for varying degrees of warmth. In short, your clothing system can adjustable for a wide range of temperatures.

While skiing, I find that on those rare occasions when I get too warm, it's usually at the end of a run. At that point, I can open my parka completely or even remove it while I'm in the lift line. As soon as I cool down a little, I can put my parka back on and/or zip it up. This way I can maintain my warmth while I'm in a chairlift, where everyone else seems to be freezing. On extremely cold days, I also wear a hood, which gets tucked out of the way as soon as I get off the lift. The hood covers my face up to my goggles, and my breath keeps my face extra warm. When a strong wind hits, even at –20° F, I feel a slight pressure from the wind but not the biting cold. It's especially gratifying to be not at the mercy of outside forces, but co-existing with them *at the comfort level I choose.*

In the past few years, I have also been using a vapor barrier shirt over my underwear clothing layer. As noted in Chapter 3, vapor barrier has some significant benefits over a breathable clothing system. It prevents moisture from my body from entering my insulation, with the following results:

- Less insulation is required because evaporative heat loss is reduced to nil;
- The humidity level at the skin is maintained high so that insensible perspiration is reduced;
- Hydration (fluid levels) are maintained during the day, thus delaying the onset of fatigue;
- Insulation remains dry and continuously effective at its peak level; and
- Insulation layers stay free of body dirt and oils, and thus require less frequent cleaning.

The third and fourth points were most noticeable to me when I first started using the vapor barrier. I was just as warm at the end of the day as when I started, and I was less tired than usual. Before using vapor barrier, if I wasn't careful about venting and let moisture build up in my clothes, I was not as warm as I wanted to be near the end of the day. For most people, perspiration buildup in insulation is the norm; together with ordinary insensible perspiration, it accounts for a significant amount of the total heat loss.

SUGGESTED SKI CLOTHING SYSTEMS

Vapor Barrier

Underwear: Try to use one of the non-absorbent materials, such as polypropylene or polyester, for all underwear. This includes the first layer on hands and feet as well as on torso and legs. Use thin underwear, not expedition weight, under the vapor barrier,

Vapor barrier: Use a vapor barrier liner on torso, hands and feet. You don't have to use it on your legs unless you're planning to ski at 10° below zero F, or lower. When you ski, your legs are the hardest working part of your body, they produce a lot of moisture which you want to evaporate. If you don't ski very hard and your legs get cold, it's fine to try vapor barrier to see if it keeps your legs warm.

Insulation: Next comes the main insulation layer (or layers). It may consist of just a sweater or ski jacket, or a few sweaters and one or more ski jackets or vests. It all depends on the effective temperature in which you expect to ski. For average ski temperatures (10°–25°F), I usually wear a bunting (polyester) sweater and an ordinary ski jacket. This is the element (thickness of insulation) to experiment with in order to fine tune your warmth. (Remember: A little extra warmth up top means more warmth for your hands and feet.) If you are concerned with looking too bulky, go for one of the thin insulations, such as *Thermolite* or *Thinsulate.*

Outer shell: The system's top layer (or shell) should be a wind-proof/waterproof material. This layer need not be separate; it can be the outer material of your parka. It should, however, contain a hood. In a vapor barrier system, the outer shell doesn't have to be one of the more expensive waterproof/breathable materials. Any totally waterproof outer shell will protect you from both wind and water, and these are usually less expensive than the waterproof/breathables.

Breathable

Underwear: The first layer of clothing should be one of the non-absorbent materials. However, in very cold conditions you might want to use a heavier, expedition-weight, material. (This isn't an advantage of the breathable system; it's just not needed in the vapor barrier system.) In either system, it's a good idea to use a turtleneck undershirt for the protection it provides your neck. Do *not* wear regular underwear under polypropylene or polyester materials. Regular underwear contains cotton which is very absorbent and will completely undermine the purpose of the poly materials. Some people like to wear a wool layer over poly underwear to trap the moisture away from the body. This is all right, but not as effective as using only non-absorbent materials, such as polypropylene bunting or polyester pile or batting.

Insulation: In a breathable system, the insulative layer serves the same purpose as in the vapor barrier system: it slows heat loss. One difference to note is that since evaporative heat loss from insensible perspiration is not handled by this system, it requires a little more insulation to provide the same amount of warmth. A more important difference between the two systems is that the type of insulation used in the breathable system is more critical than in the vapor barrier system. Insulations such as down or wool can absorb a lot of moisture and greatly reduce the value of the insulation. I would stick to using only man-made poly materials in the insulative layers of a breathable system. The hollow-fiber materials, such as *Quallofil* and the other polyester battings, are advantageous because they don't absorb any moisture in the fibers. Pile or bunting sweaters are excellent as insulation, as are polyester batting ski jackets and vests.

Outer shell: Tightly knit nylon material will block the wind to a large degree, but for the protection a skier really needs (especially in a breathable system), I would use one of the waterproof/breathable materials such as *Gore-tex*. The extra wind protection afforded by these materials can make a big difference in warmth. Again, it pays to have your entire outfit protected, including torso, legs and hands. Whether the outer shell is part of an insulated jacket or is separate, make sure the top can be sealed at the waist against the wind. This can be accomplished by an internal wind/snow skirt or an elastic band at the waist. If the waist is not sealed against wind, the convective heat loss (from the "chimney effect") can be great.

MORE HOT TIPS FOR SKIERS

Neck: Protect it with a turtleneck shirt or sweater, or a neck gaiter. Some stores now sell a polypropylene neck gaiter which can be pulled up to cover part of your face. Never wear a scarf (or any loose hanging material) while skiing. More than one person has been snagged by a chairlift or a rope tow because of a loose scarf.

Head: Always wear a hat while skiing. Your heat energy loss without one is enormous. Most skiers use a tightly knit wool hat, but there's a way to make a dramatic improvement in head warmth. Either buy or make your own liner cap out of tightly knit nylon or, even better, *Gore-tex*. Buy a *Gore-tex* lined watch cap and either sew the liner into your ski hat or just wear your ski hat over the liner. If they are separates, try this experiment: On a cold windy day, wear your regular ski hat while riding the lift up or skiing down; about halfway up or down, quickly put the liner under your ski hat and complete your ride up or your run down; the difference in warmth will be immediate and dramatic. You may never want to ski without this combination again.

Food: Make sure you eat well and drink liquids (but no alcohol). Your body needs the fuel for warmth, and your body's fluid level has a direct bearing on its efficiency.

Feet: **THICKNESS = WARMTH** is also true for ski boots. Stay away from super-thin ski boots; they won't have enough insulation. Compare the thickness of the bladder/lining in boots you're considering. Almost all of a boot's insulation is in the lining, so it's likely that the thicker the lining, the warmer the boot. Also look in the foot bed under the lining. Some newer boots are using *Thinsulate* or foam to fill this previously empty area; these will be warmer boots.

Boot covers (or gaiters) made of foam can add ten to fifteen degrees of extra warmth to your feet, so don't ignore them; they can provide comfort on a horribly cold day. If you use vapor barrier for your ski boots, make sure you get a proper fit, wearing the vapor barrier liner and the socks you will use when skiing. If you wear only a thin sock when skiing, it probably won't do much good to use a vapor barrier. If you use more than one pair of socks, or a thick pair of socks, then a vapor barrier should keep you warm. Don't add a vapor barrier to your existing boot/sock combination if your feet don't have plenty of room; constricting the blood flow could make your feet much colder and wipe out any benefit of the vapor barrier.

Alternatives: If you're not dressed well enough for existing conditions, it's better to occasionally retreat to the warm lodge than to shiver your way through the day. Another way of warming up is to do isometric exercises when you're in the chairlift or standing still. Using various muscle groups in a few minutes of isometrics is much better than windmilling your arms, as some people like to do. The former directly increases your warmth while the latter can lose more heat than it creates.

DRESSING FOR ACTIVE SPORTS

Runners

Runners usually put out consistently high energy and therefore need much less insulation in a given temperature than people involved in less vigorous activities. This is because the high energy output also produces high heat buildup in the body. (Remember: the muscles are only one-third efficient; two-thirds of the energy they produce is "waste heat," which the body must get rid of). For runners to dress comfortably for different conditions may require a lot of fine tuning, since they wear comparatively little insulation in cold temperatures.

A standard running outfit might be just a T-shirt and a pair of running shorts. When the temperatures go below 50°F, a runner should increase upper-body insulation. Probably the best piece of gear for this is a thin (polypro or polyester) zippered turtleneck shirt. It provides additional warmth under the T-shirt, but it can be adjusted at the neck, and its sleeves can be pulled up easily for extra ventilation.

When temperatures dip to the low 40s or high 30s, the standard running suit (or warmup suit) is added. This usually is a thin acrylic or polyester/cotton combo of matching top and pants. Pure polyester is the best material for a running suit; cotton is the worst, due to cotton's high water absorbency. The running suit allows venting with a front zipper and a zippered turtleneck. At these temperatures, gloves may be needed, although some people don't seem to need them until it gets even colder. If gloves are not worn at less than 50°, I recommend that petroleum jelly or a skin cream be used on the hands.

For windy conditions, or for more warmth, a thin nylon windbreaker can be worn over the warmup suit, and windpants can be added as well. For all around conditions, including wet and windy, many runners prefer a *Gore-tex* suit, or an equivalent windproof, waterproof, breathable wind-suit. When temperatures get to the low 30s or high 20s, a cap should be used. Knit caps are best if they're large enough to cover the ears.

When the temperature goes to the low 20s and into the teens, a runner should add thermal (polypro) bottoms under the warmups, as well as adding extra insulation up top. Thermal underwear comes in regular and heavy weight so you can wear the thickness you need, or even double up thicknesses. There also are running outfits that are thicker than the normal for extra warmth. *Gore-tex* mittens can be worn over gloves to keep the hands protected, and knit hats can also be bought with *Gore-tex* liners.

When the lower teens are reached, it's time to add a face mask (neoprene is good). Some people get away with just face cream, but a face mask is much warmer. If your feet need extra warmth, you should buy all-leather running shoes which are warmer.

The best gear to use in very low temperatures is a vapor barrier shirt over a polypro turtleneck. (I start wearing the vapor barrier at anything below +30°F). This allows you to wear less on top, but the real treat comes after the run. During a cool-down walk, you don't have to worry about sweat in your outer layers cooling you off too much or for too long, because there is no sweat buildup in the outer layers when a vapor barrier is worn. You can sweat under the vapor barrier, but it can be vented as needed. Runners who don't run more than 20 minutes or so won't usually build up as much heat as those who run longer. Shorter runs, therefore, may require more insulation.

For those on a tight budget, don't bother about the fancy stuff. Just pile it on until you're warm enough — and run! Time your cool-down walk so you're back home before you get cold, and walk a little indoors if you have to.

Cross-country Skiing

Like running, this is a very active sport, so little insulation is required even in fairly cold weather. However, a problem can occur when skiers get stranded outside, either by getting lost or by being injured. When not skiing, one can get cold very fast, and there is a great risk of hypothermia. A simple ankle sprain can quickly turn into a survival crisis for an unprepared skier. It is therefore important for cross-country skiers to carry extra insulation for use if they have to stop for any length of time. Skiers who always use a prepared track close to a lodge may need little or no extra gear. However, if you ski into the woods, you always should carry a small pack with survival gear. This should include a plastic vapor barrier suit, down jacket, breath mask, very thick hat or hats, a closed-cell foam pad to sit or lie on, and mittens; insulation for legs and feet is also advisable.

Ice Fishing

Wear vapor barrier over underwear; wear thicker clothing than you think you need and take something off if you are too warm; wear more on your head than you are used to; and be sure to keep a thick foam pad under your feet and your bottom.

Street Vendors

Wear more clothing than you think you'll need; wear a thick hat or hats; stand on foam or an inch-and-a-half layer of dry cardboard, newspapers or magazines.

Fishermen, Sailors, Kayakers, Canoeists, etc.

Wear only non-absorbent underwear such as polypropylene or polyester, with turtleneck top; wear vapor barrier over the underwear; wear only foam or poly insulations; wear insulation thick enough for warmth at your activity level; wear a totally waterproof outer shell. There is a special outer shell for kayakers; it consists of waterproof material with neoprene closures at wrists and a hood with neoprene closure around face. One supplier is Patagonia in Ventura, California; another is Recreational Equipment in Seattle, Washington.

Bicycle Riders

- Protect the neck area with a turtleneck or dickey.
- In very cold conditions, block the vents in hard-shell helmets; a polyester or polypropylene balaclava will further protect head, ears and neck.
- Wear sunglasses or goggles to protect eyes from prolonged exposure to cold winds.
- Coat your face with petroleum jelly (it's better than face creams) to help protect your skin; in very cold conditions, use a foam ski mask.
- Wear windproof/waterproof insulated gloves.
- Use insulated, waterproof shoe coverings, which are available from bicycle specialty catalogues; waterproof rain capes that attach to the handlebars are also available through these catalogues (see Appendix 3, Resources).
- Wear a windproof, waterproof, breathable outer shell both top and bottom.
- Wear thermal underwear both top and bottom. (Knees can get very cold since they are always directly facing the wind).
- Adjust the thickness of your insulation under your outer shell to keep you warm. (Pumping the pedals faster will also produce more warmth).

When you start out, dress on the cool side so you don't overheat when your muscles start pumping out calories. If you're still cold after five or ten minutes of riding, it's time to add insulation. If you overheat, you'll sweat into your insulation, and this diminishes its value as an insulator and may cause you to cool down much too quickly when you slow down. A vapor barrier shirt would prevent sweat from contaminating your insulation; it may be an excellent piece of clothing for cold-weather bicycling.

Picketing in Cold Weather

Use poly underwear (with turtleneck top) and vapor barrier over that. Wear an appropriate thickness of insulation: more than one sweater or few ski jackets or vests. Pile it on until you are warm enough. You can still move your arms around and blow on your hands to make people think you are cold. Being bundled up makes you look cold; nobody has to know that you're warm as toast, and you don't have to tell them. Important: Keep your head and neck warm; you can lose more heat here than you realize.

HINTS FOR DRESSING WARMLY IN THE CITY

In cold weather, city dwellers are frequently worse off than people in rural areas. Because we're used to being indoors most of the time, traveling between two buildings across town seems like an expedition during cold weather. I see many people who are inadequately dressed for the cold. They feel helpless against the cold; they never suspect they're wearing too little insulation. Another problem is fashion. People seem to opt for fashion over warmth, but the two don't go well together when the mercury plunges to the teens and lower.

There's really no such thing as an "all-weather coat." Even if a man is wearing a suit, his lined "all-weather" coat (or trench coat) is adequate only down to about the 30s. Below that, thicker insulation is needed. It's that simple. A heavier wool overcoat will be warmer, but a thick lining should be installed in it when the thermometer drops to the teens or lower.

Hats are also poorly designed. The only urban hat I've seen that is warm enough for very low temperatures and still fashionable is a thick fur hat which covers the ears. Since these are quite expensive, an alternative would be to line the inside of a regular man's wool felt dress hat with a half-inch to an inch of *Thermolite* or *Thinsulate*; a hat of this type would also require the use of earmuffs. A good wool scarf should always be included in very cold weather, since it can be pulled up to protect the face. For the elderly, or anyone bothered by cold air, breathing through a scarf can protect the throat and lungs in extreme cold; at least two layers of material should be used for this.

For women the choice of coats is greater, but the results are unfortunately the same. Many women either don't want to wear thick enough insulation to stay warm, or they don't know it exists. Many of the coats women wear are not the least bit windproof; for a coat to be windproof, it needs a tightly woven lining in most cases. Among the warmest coats for women are the long, thick polyester or down-filled coats with a tightly woven nylon outer cloth and a high collar. These are like a ski jacket turned longer and fancier for city wear. Too bad they couldn't do the same thing with men's trench coats! (The closest thing I've seen for men is a down coat.) Fur coats are also very warm. But getting back to basics, fake fur is just as warm as the real thing if it's as thick and the lining is windproof. If it's thicker, it's warmer. (Now you can give the animals a break and save money, too!)

Best for keeping hands warm in the city are insulated gloves with either a nylon or leather outer shell. The insulation should be one of the thin types, such as *Thermolite* or *Thinsulate*. This type of glove is just slightly thicker than uninsulated leather, but much warmer. Both men's and women's gloves are available with this insulation.

Hints for Dressing Children

An important point to remember about children is that their small bodies have a higher ratio of surface-area-to-volume than adults. Accordingly, they lose heat more quickly than adults and therefore need more insulation to stay warm in the same conditions. Smaller children don't always know how to communicate just what is bothering them. If they feel cold, they may just cry or whimper without communicating specifically what's wrong. Parents should check periodically whether their child's skin feels cold. For children who can communicate, it may be best to provide them with adequate insulation and let them adjust it themselves once you've taught them how to stay warm.

In cold weather, children should be provided with a hooded jacket. The hood should not be just for looks, but should contain insulation. Older children may not want to use the hood, but if they get cold enough, they will. In very cold weather, a knit cap, a hood and a scarf make good sense.

Mittens are warmer than gloves. It's not a bad idea to pin them to the jacket sleeve. Better yet is a length of string tied to one mitten, run up one sleeve then down the other, tied to the other mitten. This allows the mittens to be quickly removed without being lost. If your child complains about it, you can explain that all the best mountaineers do the same thing so they won't lose a mitten on a huge mountain. (It's true! A lost mitten on a cold mountain can mean losing a hand, or even a life.)

Make sure the child's jacket has a tightly knit nylon outer shell for protection from the wind. Most cotton materials are too loosely knit for an outer shell and will allow the wind to whip through. Also make sure children's shoes fit well and are not tight. Any constriction will cause cold feet. Shoes with thick foam soles should generally be the warmest.

Keeping the Face Warm

In very cold weather (below 15°F), any exposed area of skin is subject to rough treatment. Usually the face is left uncovered and thus open to the ravages of the weather. When it's very cold, it's usually also very dry. The skin reacts by pumping out moisture to protect itself from drying out; this moisture evaporates quickly in the dry air, causing additional heat loss. When this cycle is at work, the face becomes dry, cracked and susceptible to frostbite.

One way to protect your face in cold temperatures is to wear skin cream; petroleum jelly is the least expensive and best for the job. It must be thick enough to cover the pores of the skin. This will prevent the evaporation of moisture and its cooling effect. Skin cream provides only partial protection, however, because moisture in the skin, as well as the skin itself, can still get cold enough to cause frostbite.

Depending on your own sensitivity, there's a point when you will want a face mask for protection against the onslaught of the wind. Face masks are available in a variety of materials and configurations. There are knit, hooded ski masks and balaclavas, as well as masks made of foam, leather or even insulated leather. You can even buy down-filled face masks.

My preference is the neoprene foam face mask which I use mainly for skiing, but it also comes in handy for hiking and camping. It's small enough to fit in a pocket when folded, so it's very handy.

Another form of face protection is the elongated hood on snorkle parkas. It extends out about six inches from your face, creating an air pocket which resists being whipped away by the wind. This air pocket retains some of the warmth of your breath and skin and thus helps keep your face warm.

Keeping Hands Warm

It's important to remember that your hands are integral parts of your body. If your body is warm, your hands may be either warm or cold depending on how well you've insulated them. However, if your body is cold, it's next to impossible for your hands to be warm even if they're well insulated; your cold body will reduce blood flow (and therefore heat flow) to its extremities in order to preserve heat in its core. Insulation by itself provides no warmth; it only slows the rate of heat loss.

One evening at the Tanglewood Music Festival in Massachusetts, the temperature dipped to 40°F, much lower than most audience members had expected. I overheard a woman in back of me saying, "I swear my hands are colder with my gloves on than with them off." I glanced at her gloves, thought briefly about her comment, and realized that she was right. Her senses were telling her the truth, but she didn't believe them. She was wearing very thin black gloves. Factors working against the woman benefiting from wearing the gloves were the gloves' color and the fact that they were so thin as to provide almost no insulation. Black is the color with the greatest rate of heat radiation; the woman's black-clad hands were radiating heat faster than if she had the gloves off. The thin black gloves definitely caused her hands to be colder, but she left them on because she believed that wearing gloves *should* keep them warmer. (I kept quiet; it wasn't exactly a survival situation, and the music was too good to interrupt.)

Assuming your body is sufficiently insulated and warm, what does it take to keep your hands warm? For mild outdoor cold, sometimes just a pair of knit gloves is sufficient. When colder conditions prevail we must again look at our three adversaries: **cold, wind** and **water**. To protect against cold temperatures, we need **thickness** in insulation. For wind, we need a windproof outer covering, such as tightly knit nylon or leather. For moisture protection, a waterproof/breathable fabric (*Gore-tex* or equivalent) will keep your gloves or mitts dry. (*Gore-tex* laminate is also an excellent wind barrier, much better than just nylon.)

For more protection from bitter cold (below 15°F) and for longer periods outdoors, we need to protect against body moisture (sweat). This calls for use of a vapor barrier inside gloves or mittens. This is easy to get. Just go to your supermarket and buy a pair of thin latex dishwashing gloves. Make sure they're not tight. That caution applies to any glove or mitten you wear in the cold. They should not even be snug; just barely touching the skin is fine. To ensure warmth, never restrict the circulation in your skin.

This brings us to the warmest combination of materials for hands: first a thin liner glove of polyester or polypropelene for comfort; then a vapor barrier glove to keep the insulation dry from the inside; then a thick mitten (or glove) for insulation; and finally a windproof/waterproof material to stop both outside moisture and the wind.

What about the idea that mittens are warmer than gloves? Today's gloves made of *Thermolite, Thinsulate* and *Gore-tex* laminates can be warmer than some of yesterday's mittens. However, if gloves and mittens are made of the same materials and are equally thick, the mittens will *always* be warmer. By separating your fingers in a glove, you increase the area of heat loss, and therefore the amount of heat loss; it's that simple.

Micro-fiber insulations, such as *Thermolite* by DuPont and *Thinsulate* by 3M, are standouts for keeping hands warm. In a thin layer, micro-fibers are about twice as warm as most other insulations, including down. It's best to use a vapor barrier and a waterproof outer shell when using micro-fibers, because they are harder to dry than regular polyester insulations. Down is even worse. I once wore a pair of down mittens while skiing. In the morning, my hands were warm and comfortable; in the afternoon, they became very cold, and I was miserable. They didn't get wet from the snow but from my perspiration, which soaked the down and destroyed its insulating capability. I never wore them again. (At the time I didn't know about vapor barriers.)

Many outdoor activities require occasional acts of manual dexterity that are not possible if you're wearing mittens or even thick gloves. This is another reason to wear thin liner gloves inside your outer gloves or mittens. Hands clad in thin liner gloves can usually accomplish necessary manual tasks. Moreover, without them, the danger of frostbite is greater. They also reduce the risk of getting your skin ripped off if you happen touch frozen metal; moisture in bare skin can weld it to metal. Pity the poor people who have ripped skin from their tongue by trying to warm a car key in their mouth.

One of the most dangerous threats of frostbite to hands is the accidental spilling of a volatile liquid in very cold conditions. If gasoline or alcohol is left outside, it can cool down to the coldest night air temperatures, and by being insulated with blown snow, it can remain at those temperatures. If someone tries to pour such a liquid into a stove and spills it on himself, the extreme low temperature of the liquid, combined with its rapid evaporation rate, can suck the heat right out of the skin. The temperature of the skin might drop to $-100\,°$F in a second or two, causing a serious case of frostbite which could result in some loss of flesh. Obviously, immediate medical attention is necessary. Anyone pouring volatile fluids (such as gasoline, alcohol, dri-gas, paint thinner, etc.) in very cold weather should exercise *extreme caution.*

Raynaud's Disease

Some people have a physical disorder that makes it extremely diffi-cult for them to keep their hands warm. The condition is Raynaud's disease (also called "blue fingers"). It is a localized overreaction to the cold via vasoconstriction: actually, a spasm of the blood vessels. The circulation is cut off, causing fingers (or toes in some persons) to turn blue. The disorder seems to affect more women than men.

One way of dealing with it is to keep the affected area as warm as possible by:

- Keeping the trunk, head and neck areas *very* warm to get extra heat to the extremities;
- Using the super warm combination of layers listed previously (thin liner, vapor barrier, thick mitten and waterproof outer shell);
- Making sure the layers are not too tight. You might buy mittens two sizes too large and fit another pair inside them (but not too tight). If you're concerned about looks in this case, it might cost you a lot of pain. My own preference would be to choose the puffy look.

Electrically warmed mittens (battery-operated and safe) are sold in some stores and catalogues. Although I usually don't recommend them, if they help in this condition, I'm all for them. Another route to try is your doctor. Many patients with Raynaud's disease can be helped by the drug Nifedipine or nitroglycerine ointment, both of which dilate (open) the blood vessels. This improves circulation in your hands so they can get warmth from the blood flow.

A possible cure for Reynaud's disease was reported in *The New York Times* on January 19, 1988. Dr. Murray Hamlet of the Army's Research Institute of Environmental Medicine told of a treatment first used about ten years ago by an Army doctor in Alaska. The treatment involves placing the patient's hands in warm water while the rest of the patient's body also is warm. Next, the patient is put in a cold environment, but the hands remain in the warm water. The treatment is repeated a number of times a day, every other day for about fifty days. Essentially, the treatment retrains the body so that the hands don't have such a severe response to the cold. After this treatment, all of the 150 subjects tested by the Army were able to go into cold environments without losing circulation to their hands. The treatment is being used by some doctors, but it may not be for everyone. It is very time-consuming, and if the disorder was caused by trauma or disease, the treatment might not work.

Keeping Feet Warm

In many winter travel circumstances, feet are the hardest part of the body to keep warm. This is because they lose heat through conduction by direct contact with a solid substance such as the cold ground, snow or ice. The better the insulation between your feet and the ground, the warmer they will be.

One of the principles cited in the section on hands also applies to feet; the body be must warm if the feet are to be kept warm. If your body's core temperature drops, the body will shut off circulation to the skin and then to the extremities. Hands and feet suffer first. But if your body is slightly overwarm (but not so warm as to cause sweating), it opens up circulation to the skin and tries to get rid of the excess heat through the extremities. Thus, your hands and feet stay warmer.

Another difficulty in keeping feet warm is that most people don't bother to wear much on their legs, even on the coldest days. We bundle up on top, but never think to wear anything of similar thickness on our legs. One of the largest arteries in the body, the femoral artery, is located on the inside of the thigh close to the surface; if that area is not insulated, your warm blood can be cooled considerably on its way to your feet. Most of us don't need 2"-thick expedition overpants; however, a pair of dungarees or thin dress pants are inadequate when the temperature drops to zero. Depending on the weather and your activity level, insulation may well be appropriate for the legs.

An old adage of mountain-men is worth repeating here: *"If you want to keep your feet warm, wear a hat!"* Even if your trunk and legs are adequately protected, you may be losing more than 75 percent of your heat output through your head if you don't wear a hat. Most people wear thin hats. They increase the noticeable comfort in the immediate area of your head, but they don't significantly reduce the heat loss from the head. So to paraphrase another adage, "Two hats are better than one" if one can fit over the other without being too tight (two wool knit caps, for example). A thick fur hat is also warm; even better is a thickly insulated parka hood which also protects the neck and ears. There are many types of hats available, but remember: **thicker is warmer**. The point is to reduce heat loss through the head, conserve the heat and send it to the extremities.

If your head, neck, torso and hands are well dressed for warmth but you have inadequate insulation on your feet, odds are they're pretty cold. Sherpas in the Himalayas can get away with bare feet, but we've gotten a bit too soft for that sort of thing. We need to wear footgear that's appropriate for our activity.

Some shoes and boots are sold in regular and insulated models. The insulated ones are usually better for winter. I say *usually* because some less expensive boots made for city wear are lined with synthetic woolly material (it looks like sheep wool) which may mat down after the first few times the boots are worn. This means you have to wear another pair of socks in them, which you could have done in the first place by buying boots about one size larger. This is less expensive, but we don't always think of these things when something *looks* warm and cozy in the store window.

Some of the better winter shoes and boots are insulated with foam or *Thinsulate* and have a thin lining between the insulation and the foot. Some are made with waterproof outers for really foul weather. Even these can get moisture in them from the inside. The moisture from your feet replaces the air in the insulation; this moisture transfers heat away from your feet much more quickly than air. This is a major cause of cold feet. The only way to prevent moisture buildup is for both the outside and the inner lining to be totally waterproof. This means using vapor barrier liners.

For city wear, if you're outdoors for only an hour or so at a time, vapor barriers are not necessary. But if you're outside for longer periods, whether active or sedentary, vapor barriers for the feet make a lot of sense. For some people it might take a little time to get used to, and be comfortable with, vapor barrier. Since the moisture from your feet can't pass through the insulation, your feet stay very moist yet are much warmer. A very thin liner sock (of polypropylene, polyester or wool) between your foot and the vapor barrier should prevent the soggy feeling.

Now that your body is warm, your head and legs are protected, and you have a vapor barrier sock in your boots, are your feet warm? Well, maybe and maybe not! It's now up to the insulation around your feet to keep your feet warm. This insulation can be in one or more of four types:

1.) **Built-in, as foam or synthetic liner:** Some shoes and boots are made with built-in insulation, which can vary in thickness. Some manufacturers are making boots with a double thickness of *Thinsulate.* Foams are also good and are used in some of the best mountaineering boots.

2.) **Removable liners:** Socks are the standard example. You can buy shoes or boots a bit too large in order to accommodate the thickness of socks you want to wear. When you're shopping for shoes or boots, you should wear the sock combination you intend to use, or you might not get the fit you want. If the shoes are too tight, they will constrict the circulation in your feet and you can kiss warmth goodbye. If your activities include much use of the feet, such as hiking, snowshoeing or cross-country skiing, you should allow for the expansion of the feet due to the activity. Usually at least one size larger than your normal street shoe size is necessary. If this is not taken into consideration, you could be setting yourself up for frostbite due to the constriction of blood flow in the feet. Another type of liner in some winter boots is made of wool felt. Liners are also available in neoprene and other foams as well as a *Gore-tex* and *Thinsulate* combination. All liners, especially socks, should be kept clean. Any dirt, water or body oils will quickly reduce the insulative value of the liners.

3.) **The sole:** This is an important area of the shoe from the standpoint of warmth. Thin leather or plastic soles cause you to become very aware of your feet in winter. This is due to the pain caused by the cold before numbness sets in. The thicker the sole, the warmer the shoe (assuming the sole is an insulator and other things are equal). Soles in running shoes are thick foams which absorb the shock of running. Since foam is a good insulator and since these soles are thicker than average, they are much warmer than average. Manufacturers realized the potential of this type of sole for hiking and hunting shoes and began using it not long ago. Even more recently, foam soles began showing up in "walking" shoes. These shoes are for exercise walking, but some people buy them because they are as comfortable as running shoes and give better lateral support. A few manufacturers even make decent looking dress shoes with thick foam soles. They might not be totally acceptable for business, but they can get you to the office in warmth. Once at the office you can change to your dress shoes. (Seems women found out about this trick several years ago. Many women use running shoes to get to work. They find them warmer and just a tad more comfortable than high heels.)

4.) **Overboots, boot covers or boot muffs:** There are many activities which have their own type of footwear, and many of these have some type of after-market overboot designed for them. Plain or insulated overboots are available for the following specialized shoes and boots: hiking, climbing, skiing, cross-country skiing, bicycling and others. The overboot is usually made of a sandwich of materials; typically they have a thin nylon inside and strong nylon outside with some type of insulation between. Some manufacturers use a *Gore-tex* outer shell to provide waterproofing and better wind resistance. Still another type is made mostly of neoprene. The overboot is used only when the weather is below about 10°F. It is an example of the layering principle applied to the feet. And it works! Most overboots add protection only to the upper part of the boot, not the sole, but when it's zero degrees and windy outside, this extra protection makes a difference you can really feel.

5
WINTER CAMPING

Many winter landscapes are so breathtakingly beautiful that they tempt summer campers to extend their trips into this season of quiet white beauty. It's impossible to fully describe the beauty, majesty and peacefulness of mountains in winter, nor can words adequately express the ferocity and danger of winter weather in the mountains. The actual winter camping experience, as well as most other winter outdoor activities, is much more valuable than mere description. Learning how to travel and camp safely in a winter environment is well worth the effort expended.

Although the lure of winter's beauty is great, the dangers awaiting the uninformed camper are also great. In the interaction between the forces of nature and living beings, there is no *caring* in the compassionate human sense of the word. Human beings *care* about each other, about animals, about things. Rocks, trees, fire, wind, water and animals *don't care*; they just do what they do! If a person is unprepared and gets stuck somewhere freezing to death, the forces of nature continue, totally indifferent to the human tragedy. A human being is solely responsible for his/her own survival in natural environments which often are unsupportive of human life.

In order not to paint too bleak a picture of the dangers involved in winter camping, I should say immediately that it's a rewarding experience which can be enjoyed fully. To cite just one example: Gil Phillips, who lives in New Mexico, enjoys camping in Alaska, and he relishes it most when the temperature hits –30°F. It's claimed that at –40°F he's able to sleep in the snow, without a tent! He makes good use of foam insulation and obviously knows the basic principles of warmth. If he (and many others) can camp at temperatures below zero, surely the average camper can learn to camp at temperatures below freezing (32°F).

On one winter camping trip I made, the temperature rose to 25°F. Even though this is seven degrees below freezing, it seemed like summertime to me, because my equipment was capable of protecting me against much lower temperatures. This shows what's possible with the right equipment and knowledge.

A camper at sea level who underestimates his clothing needs in summer might experience considerable discomfort; a similar mistake in fall or winter, or at higher elevations, could prove fatal. High mountains do not make the distinction we call "summer"; for example, on July 6, 1986, while it was swelteringly hot in most U.S. cities, a foot of snow fell in the mountains of Oregon. The highest temperature ever recorded at the top of Mount Washington, which is only about 6000 feet high, is only 72°F. Winter weather on this mountain is so brutal that, as in other severe winter environments, an unprotected person can die in less than an hour.

Winter camping requires more planning, preparation and practice than summer camping. It's strongly recommended that you be familiar with summer camping before going camping in winter. Your first winter camping should be done only a few yards from your house or a lodge; mistakes or oversights can be corrected without any real danger, not even the annoyance of losing a night's sleep. After a few nights' practice in cold conditions, you'll develop confidence in your ability to handle the cold. Anyone who doesn't practice before going winter camping is, in my mind, more than foolhardy.

If you intend to do much traveling outdoors, preparations should include endurance exercises. Whether you hike, snowshoe or ski in winter, your energy output will probably be greater than for comparable exertion in summer. If you're in good physical condition for your activity, you'll tire less easily, and you'll enjoy yourself more. Also, your body will be more efficient in utilizing the food you eat to maintain body heat.

Planning should include listing equipment you'll need, checking weather forecasts, becoming familiar with the routes you'll take, estimating the time necessary to reach destinations, and gauging the amount of fuel you'll need to melt snow for water and the amount of food you'll need for warmth and nutrition.

The amount and type of food depend on the nature of the trip. If you're just going for a weekend at lower elevations, then an ordinary variety of food is fine. Extended trips should include more fats to meet the increased energy demands of winter travel. Five or six thousand calories per day is not unusual for winter travelers. At higher altitudes, above, say, 14,000 feet, most people can't tolerate fats, and even protein is difficult to digest. So mountaineers should rely more on carbohydrates with a minimum of protein and fats. At higher altitudes people actually have a craving for sweets; these should be supplied if only to help in eating the rest of the food. At higher elevations, eating is chore and not a pleasure. Your body sends signals that it doesn't want to eat, but it needs the food and water and you must force yourself to consume them. Not to do so would decrease your available energy and increase your risk of cold injury.

Planning also should include reading books about winter camping to get information on route finding, types of travel, avalanche danger, general advice, etc. This book is concerned only with warmth, and even in that category, other books may give you tips I've missed.

Once you've determined the area where you'll be camping, selected the range of your activities and researched the lowest expected temperatures, then you can choose your gear. All of it should be sturdy, because money can't replace a critical item if you're in the middle of nowhere. You don't want to create a survival situation because you've brought only an inexpensive summer tent which can't take more than a 10 mph breeze.

Remember: **It's much easier to stay warm than to rewarm once you've let your body cool down.** Staying warm merely requires knowing what to do and doing it. Rewarming can require finding good conditions (such as getting out of the wind and/or precipitation), increasing your insulation, eating food and hot drinks, doing isometric exercises and having the time (sometimes hours) to get your body back to its normal temperature.

Insulation

For winter camping, I recommend synthetic, non-absorbent insulations (such as silicon-treated polyester and polypropylene) because they're safer than other fibers. These two polys are harder to get wet because the fibers don't absorb water. If they do get wet by retaining water between the fibers, they are much easier to dry out than down. You can increase the safety of down by using a vapor barrier. Even if you use a down sleeping bag with vapor barrier liner, I would recommend that you use a synthetic parka. And if you use a down parka, go with a synthetic bag. The reason is the safety factor; you never know how or when something will get soaked.

Many years ago I was camping in Canada with friends. When we set up our tents, we opened up our sleeping bags to fluff them up and let them gain their full loft (a smart thing to do). Then we set out for the day; by the time we got back to camp, it was raining and our gear was floating around half-soaked. So much for forgetting to zip the tent door (a dumb thing to do!). We all grumbled a lot, wrung things out and had a miserable night's sleep. The lesson is that even experienced campers can make blunders that can cause their gear to be soaked.

I've heard of people having their down bags soaked just from the humidity in the air. Most people never experience that, but it can happen. The point is that you are safer with the silicon-treated synthetics because they're harder to get wet and easier to dry if they do get wet. They can also be wrung out and still retain more than half of their warmth; when down gets really wet, it becomes a soggy mess with almost no insulative capability.

Water needs

A winter camper should try to drink at least four or five quarts of water per day. There are three times when a winter camper should drink water: when he's thirsty, when he's not thirsty and in between. Most winter campers don't drink enough water. Thirst in winter doesn't match the body's water requirements, so it shouldn't be relied on. Since your body's efficiency, well-being and ability to maintain warmth depend on proper hydration, it's better to err on the side of too much water than to drink too little. Most water should be taken in the morning and evening. The way to get most of your water in winter is to melt snow, using a good winter gas stove. Some campers melt an extra pint or quart of water when they cook supper so they can put it in a plastic bottle and take it with them to bed. The water bottle can be warmed and put next to your feet to give that sensitive area extra warmth. Wherever it's kept, it's available if nighttime thirst hits you; if it's not drunk during the night, it's available as soon as you arise.

One way to reduce water intake requirements is to use a vapor barrier liner for your sleeping bag and/or a vapor barrier jacket during the day. As noted earlier, vapor barrier virtually eliminates water loss due to insensible perspiration. The nighttime savings should be more than a pint of water, plus better sleep when you don't wake up to the midnight thirsts.

Elimination

Toilet needs should be handled in the morning or just before retiring if at all possible. However, nature can call at odd hours, so some preparation is wise. If you're in snow country, it's a good idea to create a path to the area to be used for a toilet. (Keep a flashlight handy!) Dig a hole about eight inches in diameter and about two feet deep, if you can. (Make sure it's not in a spot that will cause a mess in the spring because your waste will probably last that long before it thaws and break downs biochemically. Burn toilet paper if possible.) Build a small snow wall around the area about three feet in diameter and three or four feet high. This isn't usually necessary, but if you should have to use the toilet in the middle of the night and there's a raging wind or storm with below zero temperatures, you'll sure wish you had built that wind wall. In mountainous areas where there is no snow but the temperatures are really low, you can sometimes build a windbreak from rocks.

Some campers like to have a cutout in the bottom of their tent with a flap over it so they can dig a toilet in the snow for liquid wastes. Another method is to take an empty, plastic, wide-mouth bottle in your sleeping bag; after using it for liquid wastes, it can be drained in the morning. There are also clothing articles that offer protection at those vulnerable times. Some camping and mountaineering stores sell underwear suits with a built-in drop-seat. They come in two different thicknesses for different temperature ranges. You can also find thick polyester bunting pants and one-piece suits with a drop-seat. Some suits have a zipper in the crotch from front to back. It helps if the outer shell garment has a similar arrangement; this type of clothing is a must for serious winter camping, and is really appreciated when it's needed most.

Ideas for sleeping warm

Some campers eat their supper just before retiring for the night, causing the digestive system to do work, which creates extra heat. (Protein requires more work to digest than carbohydrates, so it creates a bit more heat.) A snack or a hot drink before retiring will do almost as well.

Unpack the sleeping bag as soon as the tent is set up, and fluff it up well so it will attain its full loft by the time you crawl in for the night. You want as much loft as possible because that's what preserves your warmth.

If your bag isn't too snug, you should be able to get into it with most of your clothes still on. As you finish undressing in the bag, your gyrations will help build up some heat in you and the bag. This is a good idea since the bag doesn't generate any heat of its own; it simply retains (for a time) the heat your body transfers to it.

It's a good idea to be warm when you first get into your sleeping bag. If you're cold to begin with, do isometric exercises in the bag to heat yourself and the bag.

In the morning, getting out of warm sleeping bag is not an appealing propect. It's a good idea to get your body moving by dressing while in the bag. This way you build up muscle warmth and pre-heat your clothes.

Having a roomy sleeping bag makes it possible to use extra clothing inside the bag to keep you warmer on extra cold nights. Don't use clothing that has moisture or perspiration in it. (If you use vapor barrier under your clothes, perspiration shouldn't get into your insulation.)

The old advice was never to use in your sleeping bag any clothing that you wore during the day; the reasoning is that body heat will be used to dry out the clothing, and it takes a lot of heat to evaporate even a little moisture. While this is true for clothes with perspiration in them, it's not true for dry clothes that were not worn during the day. Many people pushed the idea that you'd sleep warmer without any clothes in the bag. Remember: THICKNESS = WARMTH. Any dry clothing that adds thickness to your sleeping bag will add to your warmth. A word of caution: If your sleeping bag is too tight, extra clothes will tend to compress the insulation, which will result in little or no gain in warmth. If you add clothing on top of the bag, you should be careful of the same thing. Some garments, such as a down jacket or vest, are light enough that they won't compress the bag much.

Make sure your head and neck are well insulated. If you have a mummy-shaped sleeping bag, it should have a well insulated hood. On really cold nights only your mouth and nose need be exposed, and you can even put a wool scarf over them to breathe through.

Keeping Boots Warm at Night

If you've ever tried to put on a pair of frozen boots, you'll never let your boots freeze again. A skier can get away with it because there's usually a nearby lodge where the boots can be thawed. A winter camper doesn't have that luxury. Boots must be kept warm or frostbitten toes (maybe even *lost* toes) might result.

If boots get frozen, they can be warmed over a fire, but extreme caution should be used. Overheating can cause the boots to crack and later break apart. As an alternative, you can warm the boots with your body heat, but this takes longer, and you must be careful not to cool yourself down in the process.

Obviously, it's best to *keep boots warm in first place.*. This can be done in various ways. Some campers prefer to take the boots into their sleeping bags. If this method is used, the boots should be put in a plastic bag to keep the sleeping bag clean. Or, put your boots in your sleeping bag's stuff sack, first turning it inside-out (to keep the inside clean).

My preference is to put the boots under the bag and on top of the foam pad just under my knees. This keeps the boots warm enough and is comfortable enough for me so that I can sleep well. Try this method to see if it works for you.

Another method is to keep the boots close to the bag and, in the morning, tie the laces together and sling the boots over the shoulders and under the armpits inside the jacket. If boots are worn like this while you're in the tent making breakfast, they will warm up in a relatively short time. This is okay for cool boots, but I wouldn't want to try it with frozen ones unless absolutely necessary.

TENTS

Purpose: A tent's purpose is to protect its occupants from wind and water. It should not be relied on to provide protection from the cold.

Winter Camping

That's a job for your sleeping bag and your other insulation, even though it's generally a few degrees warmer inside a tent than outside.

Ratings: Tents are usually designated by type: summer, three-season or winter. Some three-season tents are strong enough for limited winter use, but if you're camping in rough, snowy terrain above timberline, the extra qualities of a genuine winter tent are desirable. Winter tents differ from three-season tents by having the following: snow flaps; two doors (one of which is a tunnel door); cooking vent; one or two small trap doors in the tent floor; frost liner; and vestibule. Since winter has short days and long nights, you'll spend more time in the tent than out, so you'll want as many conveniences as possible. If you don't have the bucks for a serious winter tent and you're going out only for one or two nights at low altitudes, any good, strong three-season tent should work. (For high mountains, or if you expect extreme weather, stick with a winter tent.)

Size: If a tent's weight isn't too much of a problem, it's a good idea to have a three-person tent for two people. This allows ample room for gear as well as people and is less claustrophobic. In larger parties of campers, a three-person tent for every two people constitutes a safety factor, in case a tent is damaged or destroyed. In a pinch, a three-person tent will accommodate four people a lot better than a two-person tent. If a two-person tent is used, a vestibule can usually be added to allow room for your gear. In winter, a little extra room means a lot.

Shape: In the past, the A-frame tent was the most widely used; today the best winter tents are much more aerodynamic. Credit for this is due, in no small part, to Bill Moss, who created the first aerodynamic dome shaped tents, and Jack Stephenson, who pioneered the first double sloping quonset shaped tents. They both continue to make some of the finest tents in the world.

The aerodynamic tents are stronger than A-frames because their shape allows them to repel the wind better, and they can take the wind from any direction. A noticeable difference is that there's less noise in aerodynamic tents than in A-frames. Since the aeros repel wind effectively, there's much less flapping than in an A-frame. This translates into more sleep for you. (Trying to sleep in an A-frame tent in a storm is like trying to sleep in a cheap motel with forty people partying all night in the next room.)

A-frame tents were used by campers for many years, and they can still be quite serviceable. If there are pull tabs near the center of the tent's sides, they can be tied to stakes to create more roominess in the tent and less flapping from the wind. A deep catenary cut in the ridgeline, as well as a tent that sets up tightly, are both signs of a well made A-frame that won't be as noisy in the wind as a poorly made one.

Secrets of Warmth

Color: The best color for a winter tent is bright orange. If you travel away from your tent, it's obviously important to be able to find your tent again. It's much easier to spot a bright orange tent than any other color, especially if you're late returning to camp and darkness is falling. Although a dark color will absorb heat better during the day, it also will radiate heat more readily at night; this is certainly undesirable. Since you're in the tent more often at night and nights are longer in winter, you're better off with a lighter color.

The thinner air at higher altitudes can make a dramatic difference in a tent's ability to absorb or dissipate heat. A friend reports that at 14,400 feet on Mount McKinley the free air temperature inside an orange tent went from –10°F to 95°F within minutes, as rays from the morning sun hit their tent. The occupants quickly abandoned their high-loft sleeping bags, only to discover the outside temperature was 0°F!

Occasionally a bad storm or whiteout will force you to take shelter in your tent. Winter storms can last several days, so you could be spending a lot of time in your tent. It could be depressing to spend that time in a dark tent, so here, too, a bright tent is more desirable. The only time you might want a dark colored tent is if you travel to the Land of the Midnight Sun. As you travel closer to the polar regions, there are seasons of very long days (sometimes 24 hours!) and very wintry weather. To help get sleep in these conditions, some people use an opaque tent liner to block out most of the light.

Construction: The tent should be well made and strong. This is a piece of equipment you don't want to fail! The material should be a good nylon or dacron (the latter is not broken down as fast by the ultraviolet rays of the sun.) The nylon doesn't have to be the ripstop variety, but it shouldn't be too thin. Compare a few brands.

A good indication of the quality of a tent is the stitching. A good tent should have eight to ten stitches per inch. Stitch lines should be straight, not raggedy. Areas that are subject to high stress should be bar-tacked (stitched over many times). Where the really high stresses are located (such as peg loops) or where grommets or tie-downs are attached, there should be extra reinforcing material. Seams should be the flat felled type, with the fabric wrapped around itself and the thread going through all four layers. There should be no rough exposed edges. The floor should be sewn in, waterproof, slightly stronger than the walls, and should extend up the walls at least six to twelve inches. Winter tent zippers should be made of strong nylon; metal zippers freeze too easily. (Even nylon zippers can freeze and therefore should be kept lubricated.)

The tent should come with a fly; this is a waterproof outer cover positioned an inch or two above the tent's main body. The fly can be built-in or added-on, but it should fit well in either case. The fly accomplishes a number of things: it makes the tent waterproof, slightly warmer and less prone to condensation. (It's disconcerting to get rained on *inside* your tent!)

Vents are a necessity in a tent. They, too, help prevent condensation. The best tents have high and low vents to create a fresh air flow. Even if you don't cook in your tent, a cooking vent is great to have, just for the air flow. If your tent doesn't have vents, make sure you leave the zippers open at least a bit, even in a storm if possible. People have died from the buildup of carbon monoxide in a tent; therefore, caution is required if you cook, or even light a candle, inside a tent. When carbon dioxide and/or carbon monoxide build up in a tent, you don't have any trouble breathing. You just feel tired and go to sleep, *permanently!* **Summer or winter, vent your tent!**

Poles should be made of one of the stronger aluminums, such as 7075. They should not be brittle but should bend if their strength is exceeded; this makes it possible for them to bend back and therefore last until you return. It also reduces the possibility that you'll get accidentally stabbed by a broken pole. Poles for some aerodynamic tents can be of lighter weight and less rigidity; when they give a little, the tent's profile is lowered and the wind load is reduced. The poles should always fit into metal grommets at the bottom of the tent. A material pocket without a grommet will eventually wear out (usually when you least expect it!) and your pole will sink into the snow.

Guy-lines should be used to connect tie points on the tent to anchors in the snow. Keep these lines long, about twelve to fourteen feet; sometimes you have to reach a tree, or you may have to tie onto a rock. The lines should be tied to the tent even when it's packed, to prevent their loss and to save set-up time. Guy-lines should be made of shock-cord, or have some shock-cord between the line and the anchor to absorb the pressure of wind gusts. A shock load is two to three times as rough on a material as a steady load of the same magnitude. Since gusts of over 80 mph are common in the mountains in winter, the lines are subject to the equivalent of a wind of more than 200 mph. No tent I know of (or house, for that matter) can withstand that kind of load. **Be sure to use shock cords!** Also, make sure the shock cords you use stay flexible in very low temperatures.

Anchors can be made from tent stakes, wide snow-flukes, tree branches, ski poles, skis, snowshoes, a stuff-sack filled with snow and various other items. One implement *not* to use as an anchor in the snow is your shovel; it's too important a tool and must be kept with you. If you get caught in a heavy snowfall, you will need the shovel to get snow off the tent, or maybe even to dig out in the morning. For camping on hard ground, some eight to ten inch nails can be useful (aluminum tent pegs will break in hard ground). You can also tie onto strong trees or solid boulders.

Special Features

Second door: A good winter tent has this for a number of reasons. It is designed as a tunnel entrance; thus, when you enter or leave the tent, it protects the inside of the tent from the direct force of a storm. If desired, two tents with tunnel doors can be connected to form one large tent. Another reason for two entrances is that sometimes the wind blows much more snow against one end of the tent than the other; if you didn't guess right on the wind, you'll be glad to have two doors.

Vestibule: This is a small covered area outside the entrance which provides additional space and is especially appreciated in winter. It protects the tent when you enter or leave, so it's generally used on the entrance opposite the tunnel. It can be used to protect extra gear. (If I had a dollar for every piece of gear lost in the snow. . .) The vestibule is also useful for cooking.

Snow flaps, or snow skirt: This is material that sticks out about a foot at the floor-line all around the tent. Snow (or rocks) can be placed on the flaps to help secure the tent and keep wind from getting under the tent. (The wind's lift-strength should not be underestimated; tents have been destabilized and blown away due to wind getting under them.)

Frost-liner: This is an absorbent piece of material which is hung inside the tent from the ceiling and is almost as large as the ceiling. It provides slight extra warmth, but its main function is to absorb moisture to prevent condensation on the nylon ceiling. If you're in variable weather (such as rainy and humid before a freeze sets in), a frost liner can be very useful; likewise if you have to cook inside the tent. Some people swear by them; I find them to be a double-edged sword. After they absorb moisture, they are much heavier and, if frozen, difficult to pack. You have to hope for good weather to dry them out. Beating the frost off the nylon roof and brushing it out may be easier.

Cooking vent: This very important feature prevents moisture buildup and consequent condensation, and it helps maintain a fresh air supply.

Two trap doors in floor: One is in the middle of the tent for elimination (liquid waste only); the other, at the end where the cooking vent is located, is a place for a stove.

Cooking: This should be done inside a tent only when absolutely necessary. That means only in a storm. Usually you can carry enough food that doesn't require cooking, so the only need for the stove is to melt snow for drinking water. One set-up for a stove is a high vent at the end of the tent and a cook hole in the floor directly beneath the vent. The cook hole usually has a zippered flap. The stove should be put on a piece of stiff foam or masonite board so it doesn't sink into the snow. Another set-up for the stove is outside the main body of the tent in a vestibule. In either case, the stove should be monitored every second it's in use. A flare-up could mean a hole in the roof. A tipped stove could destroy the tent and your gear, and even *you* if you're not quick enough. *Stay alert!*

Patching: It's a good idea to carry a needle and strong nylon thread, as well as nylon patching tape for your tent. If you're careful, you can probably maintain your tent tear-free for many trips. However, if anything should damage the tent, you can't afford to wait until you get home to repair it. A spare pole is also a wise investment.

Practice Set-up: Whenever you buy or rent a new tent, it's important to learn how to set it up while you're in the comfort of your home. Once is not enough, unless you have a photographic memory. When you're out on your trip and it's below zero, you'll find that you have to take off your mittens or thick gloves to set up the tent. If you're wearing only thin gloves, you'd better know how to set up your tent quickly. Also, if there's an emergency that requires the tent, you'll need to pitch it in a hurry. You don't want to start learning how to pitch the tent in severe or emergency conditions. *Practice!*

Set-up: When you camp in snow, first stomp out a platform for the tent using skis or snowshoes. Don't set up under a tree with a lot of snow on it, or you might have it dumped on you in the middle of the night. Try to place the tent crosswise to the prevailing wind if snow is expected; this is to prevent getting the doors snowed in. It's a good idea to build snow walls around the tent to protect against high winds. If a lot of snow is falling, it may be necessary to shovel out every few hours, so that the tent won't collapse on you. Any equipment that you can't fit in the tent should be tied to the tent. It's surprisingly easy to lose things in the snow. **Remember: Take the shovel and the flashlight inside the tent**.

One final tip about tents on snow; after your tent is set up on the stomped down platform, dig a knee-deep "porch" at each entrance. Entering the tent will be much easier (you won't have to get down on your knees in the snow) and exiting is a snap; just extend your feet, bend your knees, and stand up!

SLEEPING BAGS

A sleeping bag's purpose is to maintain your warmth when you're sleeping, as well as anytime you stay in the tent in extremely cold days, or in an emergency.

How Much Bag? This depends on the kind of camping you intend to do. If most of your winter camping will be in relatively mild winter weather, say zero and above, it would be overkill to buy a sleeping bag rated at –40°F. If you're talking about a down bag, the difference could be several hundred dollars. For an occasional jaunt in colder temperatures, an overbag can be used to increase the effectiveness of your three-season bag.

On the other hand, if you intend to go high in the mountains in winter, you can forget about "mild winter weather". Mountain weather sometimes appears to be separate from weather in adjacent lowlands. You can expect the temperature to drop about four degrees for every thousand-foot increase in elevation, and the winds are almost always greater at higher elevations. I certainly wouldn't want to underestimate a mountain in winter; people have died from hypothermia in July and August on Mount Washington in New Hampshire. If you intend to camp in extreme cold and/or high in the mountains, the purchase of a sleeping bag rated at –30°F is justified, even necessary.

There are trade-offs with either system. If you use a super warm bag, you might have a hard time adjusting if the temperature goes above zero. If you use a two-bag system, you may find the extra weight annoying on a long haul. One good compromise is to use the two-bag system and rent an expedition bag if you really need it. Another solution is to have an all-around bag with different tops for different temperatures. A few of these may exist, but the only one I personally know about is made by Jack Stephenson in New Hampshire. It's called the Triple Bag because it has three tops that can be used in any combination. If you want to camp in extreme weather as well as moderate climates, this kind of bag, although expensive, is the only one you'll ever need.

How Much Loft? The loft, or thickness, of a bag determines how warm it is. Since the underside of a bag is compressed by your body weight, you need a pad under the bag to prevent heat loss. The top side of the bag has the loft to retain warmth between you and the cold air. Manufacturers declare the total loft of their bags; you need to divide this figure in half to get the loft over your body. This figure can then be compared with the charts in Chapter 2 to see if a bag will be effective for the temperatures you expect to encounter. Since a sleeping bag provides almost equal loft over your entire body, these charts are more accurate in this regard than they are for a clothing system. Still, I would consider the charts to be minimum values and add an inch or more for comfort.

Type of Insulation: The two basic types of insulation used in most sleeping bags are down and synthetic (polyester), and there are wide variations within each type. You can buy cheap down with a high ratio of feathers to down; it will be heavier and have less loft than a better grade of down. You can also buy inexpensive synthetic bags, which weigh more than the better synthetic bags. Some synthetic bags come close to the feel and compressibility of a good down bag, and at considerably less cost.

Either down or synthetic insulation can be used to make a quality winter bag. If anyone tries to tell you that only down should be considered for serious winter use, don't believe it. The successful 1986 Steger Expedition to the North Pole used synthetic bags made of *Quallofil* by DuPont, and the lowest temperature they camped in was a mere –70°F!

Specifics about insulations:

Down: The important property of down insulation is its fill-power (FP), measured in cubic inches per ounce of down. A good quality down-blend in today's market is around 550 FP. You can still locate companies using 625-725 FP down. The difficulty for buyers is that the measuring devices may be different from one company to another, and some companies use chemicals for a temporary increase in the lofting power of down. All you can do is stick to better name brands and trust their integrity. Don't be too concerned about whether the birds plucked for your bag were ducks or geese. If a duck-down bag has eight inches of loft and a goose-down bag has seven inches of loft, then the duck-down bag is the warmer one (everything else being equal). If two bags have exactly the same features and exactly the same loft, but one is heavier, then they are equally warm (and one is heavier). This means that the lighter bag has higher fill-power down, and it probably costs more. Remember: THICKNESS = WARMTH Some people say that goose down is better because it lasts longer. Others say that down lasts longer than synthetics. My own experience is that they all lose some loft after a while. I had a goose-down jacket from a good manufacturer that lost about half its loft in five years. If you treat your gear well, it will last longer, but I wouldn't expect more than seven to ten years. It can still be usable, just not for the same temperatures.

Synthetics: The better synthetic winter bags are made out of *Polarguard*, a long fiber polyester, or *Quallofil*, a short fiber polyester. Both are being used by a number of serious manufacturers. In theory, *Polarguard*, with its longer fibers, will not come apart easily and cause cold spots, but the shorter fibers will loft a little better. If they are well constructed, both function well. The *Quallofil* bags feel more like down and compress better, while the *Polarguard* bags have a slight advantage in weight if made correctly.

If I were buying a sleeping bag as of this writing, I would probably buy one made from *Quallofil*, and I definitely would choose synthetic over down. As previously noted, the synthetics are safer than down because they don't absorb moisture in the fibers. They can retain moisture between the fibers but can be wrung out, and are warmer when wet than down. They also dry much more quickly than down. Down clumps up when it gets soaked and can't be wrung out to regain its loft. These properties are not trivial when the weather is serious.

Foam: I'm not sure if foam bags are still available, but I've heard of such bags approximately two inches thick being used at -30°F. The properties of foam are similar to synthetics, and they are even easier to wring out and dry if they get wet. The problem is that the foam bags are heavier for a given warmth rating.

Shape: For a three-season bag, both of the two basic shapes, rectangular and mummy, are adequate. Some people seem to need the roominess of a rectangular bag, and in mild winter weather they can get away with it. However, for a serious winter bag, your choice should be the mummy bag (with integral hood).

Size: Never buy a sleeping bag without trying it on for size. If you're cramped in the bag, your head or feet will push against the inner fabric and compress it, and you'll feel cold in those areas. Theoretically, the closer the inside of the bag is to your body, the warmer it is. In practice however, you might want some elbow room in your bag, for a number of reasons. If the weather gets too cold for your bag to maintain your warmth, you'll want to add to your insulation by wearing your insulated parka and even pants inside the bag. If you like to move around a bit at night, you might find a tight mummy bag too confining and uncomfortable. A third and very valid reason for getting a roomy bag is for emergencies. If someone with hypothermia is put into a sleeping bag, at least one other person should be able to get inside the bag with the patient to provide vitally needed warmth.

Color: If a vapor barrier is not used on a multi-day outing, it's a good idea to have a dark color, such as black or navy, for the cover. This will allow the greatest heat absorption from the sun and therefore the fastest drying time when the sun comes out.

Construction: A number of materials used for the outer shell of sleeping bags work quite well. Some manufacturers use ripstop nylon which is stronger than regular nylon, and some use nylon/taffeta which drapes better around the body. Some bags have a *Gore-tex*/nylon laminate for the outer shell to protect against water from outside; this is somewhat more expensive.

Check a bag as you would any sewn outdoor gear. Check to see that the stitches are straight, that there are at least eight to ten stitches per inch and that no ragged edges appear inside the bag or out. Also check to see that stress areas, such as the top and bottom of zippers, are bar-tacked.

Down bags are constructed with internal baffles of various types. The sales folk like to throw the names of baffles at you (straight, slant-box, V-tube, chevron, etc.), but the type of baffle is not a critical factor. The V-tube and chevron styles tend to control down movement better at a slight cost in weight (and money). Just make sure there are no sewn-through seams (directly from one side to the other) without some material between them (the baffle). Also, fluff up the bag and make certain that the loft is fairly uniform throughout.

Synthetic bags are constructed differently from down bags. The continuous fiber polyesters, such as *Polarguard,* are sold in batts that can be sewn directly into the bag. The short fiber polyesters, such as *Quallofil,* are first sewn to a backing to keep them together and then sewn into the sleeping bag. One bag with exactly the same loft as another may have much less weight because of better sewing and design. The price usually reflects this. As with down bags, make sure that there are no sewn-through seams in a synthetic bag and that the thickness is uniform.

Special Features

Winter sleeping bags usually have the following features:

Draft tube: This is an insulated column that backs up the zipper so no draft can come through the zipper area. Some bags have a double draft tube.

Double zipper: This maintains a more even loft at the location of the zipper; more important, it's a safety feature. If one zipper breaks (it does happen), you'll be glad to have this feature.

Shoulder tube: This is an insulated tube that goes around the top of the shoulders to block forced convective heat loss when you move around (the "bellows effect"). This tube can add significantly to a bag's effectiveness.

Boxed foot: This is an enlarged foot section that prevents the toes from compressing the material above them and reducing its insulative value. Better bags also add extra insulation on top of the foot section since it's the most difficult area to keep warm. Your hands are next to your body when you sleep, but your feet are down there on their own.

Generous head area: The head of a winter mummy bag should be large enough to close around your head with just a tiny opening left for your mouth. In extreme cold you can't leave anything exposed. The sleeping bags of the Steger Expedition were built with a tunnel column extending above the face, similar to the snorkel parkas; the column of air pre-warms the inhaled air, thus adding to the effectiveness and comfort of the bag. Manufacturers would be wise to follow this example.

Mating zippers: Most sleeping bags come with a choice of either right-hand or left-hand zippers. If you and your "significant other" are buying bags at the same time, you may wish to get "one left and one right." Both occupants in zipped together bags will be warmer; there will be a warm body rather than just cold air on one side. And the range of heat-producing isometric exercises is greatly expanded.

Foam Sleeping Pads

A sleeping bag insulates you on the top and sides, but very little underneath. Your weight compresses the insulation too much to allow it to shield you from the cold ground or snow. Down bags are worse than synthetics in this regard, but both types require additional insulation under the bag. This is best provided by closed-cell foam pads. For winter use, a half-inch thick, full-length pad should be used. If you're expecting temperatures below –40°F, add a three-quarter length piece of foam under the first one.

Various types of foams are available, including *Ethafoam, Eva-zote,* and *Ensolite*. Make sure it's closed-cell, and not a type that will stiffen at low temperatures. And don't let anyone tell you that ⅜" of any particular foam is good enough for cold weather; for winter, ½" is the minimum.

Some people prefer to use thicker open-cell foams because they cushion better and are more comfortable for sleeping. I don't like to take chances in winter. With open-cell foam, there's always a chance it will absorb water and then freeze. I prefer the chances of a closed-cell foam getting wet: *Zero!*

6

THOSE IN GREATER NEED

THE ELDERLY

Here are some age-related problems that affect older persons' ability to stay warm:

As the body ages, its systems become less efficient and don't produce warmth as easily, nor do they compensate for feeling cold as quickly.

In some instances, nerve deterioration may prevent the transmission of certain external stimuli; thus, some older persons aren't even aware if their body temperature is below 98.6°F. They can suffer from the first stages of hypothermia and not even know it. Some persons might be wise to check their temperature once a week, or even daily, to be sure their temperature is normal. A sweater might be appropriate even in an average temperature room.

Some of the elderly do not eat an adequate diet, and consequently the body is hard-pressed to maintain the required warmth. Proper food and sufficient liquids are essential. Warm drinks during the day may be helpful.

Many older persons live below the poverty level and cannot afford well heated living quarters or proper clothing.

THE HOMELESS

Homeless people in large cities in the northern United States, or anywhere for that matter, are confronted with survival conditions during the winter. When the temperature drops into the teens or below and there is no room in the shelter, or no shelters nearby, survival becomes a rougher challenge than usual.

Street people have created some interesting ways to stay warm. Some sleep in doorways and bundle up in anything they can find. Some sleep on sidewalk gratings where waste heat is being given off by machinery underground. Others make tents for themselves out of cardboard boxes. Street people once used newspapers to stay warm, but that's less apparent these days. It seems as if using newspapers for warmth has become a lost art. This is a shame, because newspaper is an excellent insulator when used correctly; it's also easily obtained. And it's free; yesterday's paper is just as warm as today's, as long as it's dry.

How do you use newspaper to stay warm?

Crumple it up sheet by sheet and stuff it under a jacket or blanket, or in pants legs; or fold each sheet accordion-style and stack the sheets (alternating directions of folding) until they are thick enough to keep you warm (3-to-10 inches, depending on conditions). Newspapers won't protect you from wind or rain; they blanket you from the cold, but they aren't shelter.

Newspaper isn't the only way to provide insulation, but it's usually the least expensive and easiest to use. Old clothing from the Salvation Army or churches should be utilized if possible. Almost any fabric, if bundled in sufficient thickness, will provide warmth, as long as it's kept dry.

How do you create shelter from the wind and rain?

This requires a lot of ingenuity, but many homeless learn techniques from others on the street. Cardboard boxes may be used as tents; they can be attached to each other to make room for more than one person. Heat given off by large machines or subways and vented through sidewalk gratings provides additional warmth. Shelters provided by the communities are usually the best, but they're not always safe. It's not that the streets are safer, but some criminal types go to the shelters just to prey on the homeless.

Plastic can provide some protection from rain and snow. If large plastic sheets can be found, they can be placed over a cardboard structure so it won't get drenched and crumple. Large plastic bags (like those used for leaves or garbage) can be placed over the body by cutting holes for the arms and head. If two bags are used, one can be placed under most of the clothing and the other over the clothing to create a vapor barrier system. This traps even more heat for the wearer. Arms and legs should also be protected by plastic if possible.

Since the head is always giving off lots of heat, the best way to stop it is with lots of hats. A very thin cap covered by a plastic bag, which then is covered by as many knit hats as can be piled on — and all finally covered by another plastic bag — creates Warmth City in very cold conditions.

If foam wrapping can be found, it can be wrapped around the top of the head or other parts of the body for warmth. Foam coffee cups can be cut or ripped in half and placed inside pant legs, sleeves or jackets with good results. If they can keep the heat of the coffee from getting to your hand, they can also keep the heat of your body from escaping too quickly. Foam cups can also be cut in half lengthwise and piled up for protection against the cold ground. A thick piece of foam, like the type found on construction sites, would be even better. A one or two inch thick foam piece used for sitting or lying down can make the cold ground just a bad memory. Construction foam isn't that much softer than the ground, but it's a helluva lot warmer.

THE INDIGENT

As of this writing, there are millions of people in this country living at or below the poverty level. Many are lucky to live in well heated buildings during the winter, or they live in areas where winter doesn't bring really cold weather. Many others, however, suffer greatly from the cold in unheated tenements.

What never makes the papers is the the cost in human suffering when people have to put up with the cold. Nobody ever writes about the number of poor who wind up in hospitals with pneumonia and other ailments, because the cold had left their body's defenses too weak to protect them. Some help is provided by the welfare system, but more needs to be done.

A RADICAL BUT WORKABLE SOLUTION!

No one really has to be cold as long as information on how to stay warm is available. At least as long as newspapers are around, no one living in a freezing apartment has to be cold. Anyone who is cold can use the street people technique of crunching up newspapers and stuffing them into their clothes. It's also much easier to fan-fold newspapers to create blankets within a closed environment (with no wind) than it is to do so in the street. The paper blankets can be made any size or thickness desired. You can staple, glue, paste or tape the individual pieces together; or you can fold them together and tear a little bit and fold over to hold the papers together.

There are only two good reasons for not using newspaper to stay warm. One is ignorance of the technique. The other is that you might not look good if someone else finds out; that is, you might be embarrassed about not having enough money to use other ways to stay warm.

There are several reasons for using newspapers for warmth if you need to:

- The alternative, being cold, isn't comfortable or healthy and it weakens you;
- You can better fight a negligent landlord when you have your strength than when you are tired, weak and sick;
- You can congratulate yourself for creating what you need instead of remaining a victim of circumstances.

I wish it were another way! I wish everyone had all the necessities and everything else they wanted in life. Unfortunately, my wishes don't match reality at this time. The truth is that some people don't live in heated rooms in the winter, and they can use the above information to help stay warm.

7
SURVIVAL

A person in a cold weather survival situation can be compared with an auto accident victim who is badly wounded and losing blood. If the accident victim is conscious, he or she knows that it's important to stop the flow of blood, or death will result. A victim of the cold is losing *heat;* the heat flow from the body must be stopped, or death will result. The crucial difference is that the accident victim can see the blood being lost, but *the victim of the cold can't see the heat being lost* and may not be as alarmed about an equally life-threatening condition.

A human being can survive more than three weeks without food, a bit more than three days without water, about three minutes without air and, in a cold environment, approximately three hours without clothing. If the cold environment is water instead of air, the last figure is closer to thirty minutes; in Arctic waters, the figure can be as little as thirty seconds. People in cold climates have plenty of air (except at very high altitudes), so the critical factor in many survival situations is *warmth.*

Whenever newspapers or televisions say someone died from "exposure," they actually are talking about a person succumbing to the cold. Many of the deaths in mountaineering have been caused by the cold, after a climber has had an accident and sustained an immobilizing injury. However, a person doesn't have to go to the mountains to be a victim of the cold. A severe winter storm can strand motorists for days, resulting in more than a few deaths from cold.

There are documented cases of elderly people freezing to death in their homes after the heat was turned off when they couldn't pay their bill. In New York some years ago, an elderly couple was found dead under their livingroom rug, which they had used in a last-ditch effort to get warm. In Brooklyn in 1977, an 80-year old woman and her 77-year old brother were found frozen to death; the woman's body was encased in ice from a broken water pipe. Even though laws were changed to prevent this kind of thing, it still happens. On January 15, 1987, a woman in Newark, New Jersey, died from the cold in her apartment after the gas company shut off her gas supply. These are not isolated cases. There are many cold-related deaths that don't make the papers and many more cases of hypothermia whose victims wind up in hospitals; these stories apparently aren't "newsworthy" enough to sell papers.

Perhaps the saddest part of these tragedies is that all were preventable. Even the elderly could have survived without any money for fuel and without any outside help, if only they had possessed enough knowledge about warmth. No matter how cold their home became, a few Sunday newspapers could have saved them — without burning the papers!

BE PREPARED!

The best way to handle cold-survival situations is to prevent them. Good preparation can turn potential survival situations into merely uncomfortable circumstances; in other words, you might wind up being colder than you would like, but not cold enough to threaten your life. For unavoidable cold survival conditions, adequate preparation can increase your survival time from a few hours to many days, or even indefinitely.

Elements of preparation:

Knowledge: From books such as this one and others about your intended activity, you can learn what it takes for your body to maintain its essential warmth; you also can get information about physical and climatic conditions of the area you are going to be in, as well as the coldest temperatures you can expect.

Physical conditioning: Some kind of endurance training, such as running, biking or swimming, is excellent for training your body to keep producing energy long past its sedentary fatigue point. This is because the amount of glycogen (fuel for warmth) your muscles can store is increased by endurance exercises; the muscles' ability to remove waste products is also improved by exercise. Thus, through physical conditioning you can increase the time it takes for you to deplete your energy stores and reduce the time it takes to recover your energy. Remember, exhaustion can be a primary cause of cold injury!

Planning: This may include storing emergency provisions and gear in a house, car or boat. It may also include alternate sources of transportation, such as a small rowboat stored in the attic if your house is in a high-risk flood area, or a skimobile or snowshoes if you live in an area of periodic extreme snowfalls. If you're traveling, plan the route you intend to take, your rest stops, the time you expect to arrive, etc. Also plan to take the proper gear for an emergency bivouac.

Experience: If your intended activity is away from the comforts of civilization, first practice close to home. If you want to go winter camping, first try camping in your backyard for a night or two in very cold conditions; that way you can safely learn what works and what doesn't. If you'll be traveling in snow country and want to know how to build a snow shelter, you could also practice this close to home. It's work, but it's also fun and educational. It can be important practical knowledge if you're far from home and nature dumps a big white blanket on you.

Emergency gear: The amount and type of emergency gear you provide for yourself should be based on the worst conditions you expect to encounter. For example, emergency equipment for a house in northern Maine would be different from gear for a house in Florida. If you're going camping, the emergency gear would differ somewhat, depending on whether you intend to camp in the woods, on a beach, above treeline or on the snow. Another variable results from the transportation you use; you can take more gear if you're traveling by car rather than hiking on foot. The following section lists some cold weather emergency gear.

EMERGENCY EQUIPMENT FOR WARMTH

Extra clothing: Basic emergency gear should include additional warm clothing. You should always have more warm clothing other than what you anticipate actually needing. If you use all of your clothing to stay warm while engaging in your chosen activity, then you're unprepared for an emergency.

Extra covering for the head and neck is absolutely essential. As noted before, the head can lose an enormous amount of heat if not well insulated. Blood flow to the head is never slowed, so no heat is saved by vasoconstriction as it is in the extremities. The head has almost no fat and only an extremely thin muscle layer to act as insulation; human hair is a very poor insulator, absolutely terrible when wet! The skull is (unfortunately in winter) a good conductor of heat away from you. In a cold emergency, *the head should be insulated at least as much as the body.* You should have thick insulation (preferably two inches thick, or more) available for your head and neck.

Vapor barrier suit or metallized "space blanket" or sack (or both): The safest of all systems is one in which you wear a vapor barrier shirt as part of your clothing system in very cold weather. When this is not used, a plastic vapor barrier should be carried. Once a survival condition develops, it may not be possible to use the vapor barrier to best advantage (under all clothing), but it still can be a benefit when placed over the clothes.

Foam pad: Closed-cell foam is one of the best items of cold weather emergency gear. If you are carrying a sleeping bag, then a full-size, half-inch thick PE (polyethylene) or EVA pad is appropriate. If you are not carrying a sleeping bag, that same foam pad is *even more important.* In an emergency, you'll need it to protect you from heat loss caused by conduction between you and the cold ground or snow.

For best use in an emergency, cut the six-foot pad in half, so you have two three-foot pieces. Then fold one piece double so you have a one-inch thick pad to sit on. Fold the other piece into a double or triple layer to put behind your shoulders if you're leaning against a wall. It's also good to have an extra piece to place your feet on (if you can't fold your legs under you).

The only two survivors in the snow cave in the Mount Hood disaster in 1986 were found on top of the other victims. The people with the longest direct contact with the snow didn't survive. Since heat loss due to conduction with the ground or the snow is enormous, closed-cell foam should be considered a *must* for cold weather survival gear.

Breath mask: A cold weather mask is available from the 3M Company, and a foam mask is sold by Spenco. These items weigh about half an ounce and can have a huge impact on lowering your heat loss during an emergency.

In a survival condition, when you're inactive and trying to conserve body heat, you lose about half your heat output through breathing; you also lose water through your breath. The cold weather breath mask slows both losses considerably. This is another *must* for cold weather survival gear.

A vapor barrier suit can weigh as little as seven ounces; a foam pad weighs eight to sixteen ounces; extra insulation for the head is about six ounces; and a cold weather breath mask weighs less than an ounce. Since all are highly effective in conserving heat, no serious cold survival gear can be considered complete without these four items.

Waterproof outer clothes: In a cold emergency, there may be contact with cold or freezing rain, snow or splashing waves. Insulation loses most of its effectiveness if it gets wet. It's in your best interest to keep your insulation absolutely dry. If you use vapor barrier, any waterproof outer shell will do, but if you do not have vapor barrier, then the breathable type of waterproof outer shell is preferred.

Other survival gear which travelers may wish to carry: a plastic tube tent if a regular nylon tent isn't used; fire starter; a knife; dry matches or lighter; a sleeping bag for a group of six on a day trip (if sleeping bags are not being carried by each person); a shovel to dig a snow cave.

THE MIND

One of the basic survival tools is your mind. Many cold survival stories have noted that those who lived were not necessarily the strongest but the ones with the greatest will to survive. It's important to take a stand for life and never give up under any circumstances.

Your mind can work for you or against you, but you're always in charge whether you realize it or not. If your mind is working against you, it's difficult to realize you're still in charge; you'll have to fake it for a while. It's easy to know when your mind is working against you; your thoughts are of "not making it": of freezing, dying, etc. Your body is probably experiencing a fear reaction: heat around the neck, headache, shaking, tightness in the chest or whatever. OK, what do you do now? I don't make promises, but these steps should help:

Start *observing* your thoughts. Don't try to stop or control them; it's crucial not to believe them. But notice them. The fact that you are in charge doesn't mean you can control your thoughts each and every second.

While observing your thoughts, start doing isometric exercises: tensing and releasing various muscle groups. Tense for five to ten seconds or so and release for about the same time. Put energy in it but don't strain or cause a muscle cramp. You might have to do this for ten to fifteen minutes to get some heat built up in your body. You also have started indirectly to handle your mind by taking direct action about your situation.

Make the choice to live. Tell yourself, either out loud or inwardly: *"I choose to live!"* or *"I choose to survive!"* or any other positive idea you select at the moment. Allow yourself to feel the choice as you say it. If any emotion appears, that's fine. Allow it!

Tell the truth! Your ability to observe your current situation in detail and in its entirety can be very powerful.

Tell yourself the truth about your situation, keeping your opinions out of it. For example, don't say that the car won't start unless you're an automotive expert or the pistons are sitting on the floor. Say: "The car doesn't seem to be startable at the moment"; or "It didn't start the last time I tried it"; or whatever is demonstrably true. Don't say: "I'm freezing to death." Keep your conclusions out of this. Instead, say what's true: "I feel cold".

Tell yourself the truth about what's going on in your body: "I feel cold in my butt and my feet"; "My hands feel shaky"; "My knees are trembling"; or whatever is specifically true for you in that moment. Don't tell yourself what was going on a few minutes back, and don't add your opinions or conclusions. Be an impartial reporter and go through your whole body, top to toe. Don't try to stop or change any body feeling. Just *observe*. Some body feelings may cease just by observing them, and that's OK.

Now observe your own mind directly. Describe to yourself your present emotional state. What are your thoughts about your situation: your ideas, opinions, feelings, etc.? Observe your mental state and acknowledge it to yourself. Don't try to change anything and don't draw any conclusions. Just *observe*.

Secrets of Warmth

It's now time to *use* your mind on your situation. You may or may not feel calmed down enough to continue; whichever is OK, too. If negative thoughts start intruding while you're doing this exercise, observe and acknowledge them. Then continue.

Create two or three pictures in your mind of how you want things to be, but imagine them to be true *now*. This is really *imaging*, not imagining. You might create an image of yourself sitting somewhere nice and warm and having heat radiate throughout your body. You might create an image of a rescue team having arrived with warm clothes, etc. It doesn't matter what specific images you create, as long as they are in line with the choices you made. Hold these pictures in your mind's eye for a while. If any emotion appears at the same time, so much the better. Hold your vision and allow the emotions to be there. It doesn't matter what emotions are present. The stronger the emotion and the clearer the picture, the more potent this process is. If you have to, create some emotion to go with your imaging, such as the emotion you would feel as soon as you find out you're safe.

If negative thoughts or fears intrude while you're doing these exercises, you may think you have no control. *Wrong!* Your control is in acknowledging your thoughts, replacing them with the vision you want and holding onto that vision. Get angry if you have to, or sad, or thrilled with the challenge. But use the emotions with the images *you want!* After five or ten minutes of the process, start using your mind to create possible solutions.

Allow your mind to be aware of your situation, and allow possible solutions to come into your mind. Imagine that your mind is an antenna and solutions to your problems can enter it. Don't *try* to think of anything; just be aware of current reality and *allow* thoughts to enter your mind. Some may seem improbable. Don't throw them away; notice them, write them down or picture them in your mind's eye as possibilities.

Now use your mind to think actively! Take your current situation into account and catalogue your resources. What are the materials at hand which can be used for warmth, insulation, signaling, etc.? Is there any extra foam or polyester that you can used to increase your insulation? Are there extra socks that can be used as mittens or tucked in your jacket?

In the worst of times, sparks of ingenuity or cleverness often appear. Allow that part of you to come forward *now* and create solutions out of anything, or out of nothing! When you direct your mind, it's your most powerful survival tool.

COLD SURVIVAL SITUATIONS

Caught Outdoors

If you're hiking, skiing or climbing and you get caught outside without sufficient gear for the conditions, your first job is to seek shelter. Once you find or create a shelter, immediately take care of anyone showing signs of hypothermia. A fire should be started if possible; if you have a stove, prepare warm drinks.

Put ground cloths, foam pads or any waterproof material between you and the snow or wet ground. Insulate yourself from the cold ground as much as possible. Place the bulk of your insulation on your trunk, head and neck. You might tuck your arms inside your outer insulation and against your body. If you're limber, you might also tuck your legs under you and put your outer insulation over them. This may allow you to use thermal overpants around your body instead of on your legs. Tucking your arms and legs reduces the area of heat transfer between you and the environment and slows the rate of heat loss.

Huddle with other people. Share the warmth; it's more thermally efficient. Get outer insulation around and on top of your companions rather than between them. If you have food, eat it, and drink liquids. Don't be concerned about rationing food; you can go a long time without food. You need it *now* for warmth.

Breathe through a couple of layers of scarf or sweater material to pre-warm your breath and reduce moisture loss. When it's very cold, half of your body's heat production at rest can be lost through your breathing. In survival conditions, you can't afford such loss.

Do isometric exercises. Use your muscles consciously; it's three times more efficient than shivering and therefore conserves energy. Isometric exercises can warm you up within a matter of minutes.

You may be tired and cold, but *don't go to sleep.* Do isometrics until your entire body is warm. If you fall asleep while you're warm, you'll wake up when you get cold; if you fall asleep when you're fatigued and cold, you may never wake up.

Stuck in a Car

This isn't as rare as you might think; winter storms regularly strand motorists. Some die from the cold. Others are asphyxiated by exhaust fumes while they're using car heaters to try to keep warm. Such deaths don't happen only on isolated backwoods roads; they also occur on major interstate highways. After a major storm, it sometimes takes days for assistance to reach all the stranded vehicles.

Secrets of Warmth

Getting caught in a car in a snowstorm is, for most people, a very dangerous situation. Most of us are soft and accustomed to the creature comforts. When we're cold, we turn up the thermostat in our house or the heater in our car; when we're stuck we call a tow truck. If we get stuck in the snow, we just sit there impatiently, waiting for the snowplows to arrive; as in the movies, the cavalry is supposed to come to our rescue. This kind of complacency can lead to death. *You don't realize you're in a survival situation. What you don't know can kill you.*

The time to take action is as soon as you're stuck, not after waiting hours for help to arrive. If you merely wait for rescue, you're not likely to take appropriate action to stay warm after your gas is used up and your heater no longer works. Remember: **It's much harder to rewarm after getting cold than it is to stay warm in the first place**. When the snow is heavy enough to stop traffic on a major highway, don't count on snowplows getting through for several hours, maybe days.

An automobile isn't the best place to get stuck, but it's better than being outside because it provides protection against wind and moisture. A snow cave is warmer, but you'd be ill-advised to build one next to your car since a snow plow may crush the snow cave with you in it. Even snowed in cars have been crushed accidentally by snowplows (and bulldozers); if drifting snow hides your car, mark it with something sticking up through the snow.

Preparation: It's a good idea to keep emergency gear in your car in winter. It's smart to carry extra clothing and blankets in the back. (See pages 111–112 for other items.) Newspapers can easily be carried in a car and used for insulation in an emergency; a couple of hefty Sunday editions of any metropolitan newspaper would probably be enough to keep you warm for weeks (not by burning them, but by crumpling the paper and placing it around you). Another idea is to place thin closed-cell foam mats (such as those used as packing for furniture and stereos) under the rugs in the car. Several layers of this material can be placed front and back without being too thick or noticeable.

What to do: Unless you see shelter that you can reach easily, staying in the car is the best thing to do. If you can run the car's heater, do so for *short periods* (twenty minutes or so), and keep the windows open at least an inch. People have died of asphyxiation from car fumes even with their car windows slightly open, so don't keep the car running too long.

The metal skin of the car is a great conductor of heat (*away* from you, unfortunately). Since snow is a good insulator, it's a good idea (if you're up to it physically) to pile snow on the car if outside temperatures are below 20°F. Use a shovel, hubcap or anything you can improvise to build up the snow to a foot or more in thickness. Don't compress it or it will lose its insulative value. Remember to mark your car so it — and you! — don't get crushed by a snowplow.

If you have extra clothing, put it on before you feel cold. *Don't wait!* If you have newspapers in the car, start crumpling up the sheets one by one and place them around you. Stuff a few into your jacket, if you have room, and also in the pants legs, if possible. Put crumpled paper around you and on your lap. Place a few sheets of uncrumpled paper on top of or between layers to keep them in place. If you start to overheat, remove some paper. If you don't have a hat, make one out of paper. The heat loss through an uncovered head and neck can be enormous.

Lacking newspapers, or in addition to them, rip apart the upholstery. The foam in it is an excellent insulator and should be put around your body where it can do some good. The headliner can be ripped out and used for additional insulation around you. The rugs can be cut up and placed directly under your butt and your feet. *You may feel very silly ripping up the inside of your car. You could wind up looking awfully stupid. On the other hand, if you pass up the chance to use available insulation, you could wind up very dead! Personally, I'd rather accept the first possibility than the second.*

After you've done everything possible to insulate yourself, do isometric exercises if you're still not warm enough. This involves using opposing sets of muscles against each other, or immovable objects, for the purpose of generating heat in your body. For example, you can press your palms together hard for five to ten seconds and then relax them for the same time, or a little more. Repeat this exercise for five or ten minutes and then start on a different set of muscles. Also use your leg muscles, but don't press so hard that you cause muscle cramps. Rest a few minutes between exercises. If you don't overdo it, you can do isometrics for a long time and generate much-needed warmth. If you get tired and want to sleep, it's all right to do so *if you are warm enough and not exhausted!* When you get too cold, you'll wake up just as you do at home when you get cold. If you are very cold or really exhausted *don't go to sleep.* Keep exercising and maintain your warmth. You can always sleep after you're rescued.

If you're not alone, huddle together with the other person or persons and share body heat. Put any extra insulation around you and on top of you, not between you and the other person(s). If there are other stranded cars nearby, have three or four persons share one car rather than having one person in each car.

If you have food or drink (not alcohol) available, use it as soon as you're hungry. It will help keep you warm *NOW!* Don't worry about being hungry later; you can go a long time without food.

Lack of water takes days to cause death; lack of food takes weeks; lack of sleep can't kill you; nor can you die from people thinking that what you did was stupid. What *can* kill you in a matter of hours is the **COLD**.

Stranded in a House

People are sometimes trapped in their homes by a blizzard, then power lines go down and the heat is shut off. When floods occur during cold weather, people learn the hard way just how cold 40°F or 50°F can be. People have died indoors due to lack of heat. If you get caught indoors without sufficient heat, you should know the ways to deal with the problem. The methods presented here can help to change a survival situation into a manageable one.

Preparation: If you live in an area where cold weather is a threat, you'll be smart to prepare for the worst. Items to store might include:

Sleeping bags: If storage space isn't a big problem, a foam bag is a good all around choice since it's great in wet conditions. If cold, dry conditions are the threat, any synthetic bag will do. As an alternative, you can get a few thick polyester quilts.

Flashlights with extra batteries; also a box of candles.

Food: Keep cans of food which have a long shelf life and contain food that can be eaten from the can; keep more than one can opener. Spaghetti wrapped in aluminum and taped for waterproofing might come in handy, if you also have a small gas camping stove for cooking it. For a few days of cold conditions, food isn't as important as warmth, but why suffer any more than you have to? Also, the food can help you to stay warm.

Water is more important than food. You should keep five or six gallon jugs of water on hand. If you bottle tap water, add a water purification tablet so that germs won't contaminate it; the tablets can be purchased in camping stores. If only snow or ice is available, you'll need a gas stove to melt the ice for water; portable gas stoves are also available in camping stores.

Save a few stacks of newspapers in a high dry place, such as your attic. In normal conditions, they'll add to the insulation of your attic, and in an emergency they make great survival insulation (as long as they're kept dry).

Vapor barrier: Any lightweight waterproof rain gear will work, as will large plastic bags.

In flood-prone areas, it's a good idea to keep air mattresses and closed-cell foam insulation, such as foam life jackets or neoprene insulation.

What to do: If the time comes when you're without heat in a house, don't panic. You're in a lot better shape than if you were outdoors. If you have a fireplace, by all means use it, if possible. If you have a gas stove, *do not* use it for warmth unless you have absolutely no insulation, and the gas stove is your only source of warmth. The amount of air it uses is too dangerous; more than one person has died because of using a gas stove to stay warm indoors.

Take an inventory of all the available insulation in the house. This includes clothing, sheets, blankets, towels, rugs, mattresses, newspapers, magazines, books, pieces of foam (such as dry kitchen sponges or an ironing board cover).

If you know the situation is only temporary, close all the windows tightly and pile on enough insulation to stay snug. If you're unsure about the duration of the situation, then you should take extra steps to ensure the survival of your family and yourself. In a survival situation, you have to suspend ordinary thinking in order to allow for extraordinary possibilities. In your normal day-to-day life, you wouldn't think of tearing out all the pages in a book, crumpling them up and stuffing them inside your jacket or quilt. But in a cold survival situation, this unusual action would provide extra insulation that could be life saving.

Four or five inches of insulation is all you need to protect you from even below-zero temperatures. If you lie on a mattress and pile quilts, blankets, towels, clothing or any other kind of insulation on top of you, it won't be difficult to get a sufficiently thick insulative layer. If you're not warm enough, just pile the insulation higher. Make sure you wear some thick insulation on your head, because this is an area of great heat loss when unprotected. If you are with other people, huddle together for warmth. Put all the insulation around you, not between you.

Newspapers can be crumpled page by page and stuffed between sheets, or in a quilt cover, or under your coat. The pages can also be fan-folded and criss-crossed on top of one another. They can be taped together, or stapled, or glued, or just twisted together to form a blanket. This will have to be thicker than ordinary insulation because the air spaces are great and allow too much convective heat loss; a thickness of about twelve inches might do for 0°F.

If you need more warmth, do isometric exercises. These pit various muscle groups against each other or against immovable objects. Expansive movements are not involved, so the exercises can be done anywhere. Alternately use muscles in your arms, hands, legs and body for five to ten seconds, and rest for about the same time. Repeat as long as it takes to warm up, and again when you need more warmth. Examples of isometric exercises are clenching your fists; using your arms to press your palms tightly together; pressing your legs together; holding your arms against your legs and trying to force your legs apart; holding your arms under your legs and lifting up; etc. You can invent many more exercises, using other muscle groups.

HYPOTHERMIA

Hypothermia literally means "too little heat." In medical terms it means a lowering of the body's core temperature, resulting in the breakdown of bodily functions — and ultimately death, if left unchecked.

Hypothermia is generally regarded as a threat to anyone removed from the comforts of modern civilization. This could even be only a mile or two into your favorite hiking area, where you can't just walk into a warm house whenever you feel like it. However, hypothermia also is a real threat in civilized areas. It's a danger to anyone who falls into water in the winter; to people trapped in their cars in a blizzard; to elderly folks who can't afford the heating bill; to the indigent who live in cold tenements; and to the homeless. It's even a threat to skiers!

Most skiers aren't overly cautious about dressing warmly; they're willing to put up with feeling a little cold in order to enjoy their sport. If relatively lightly dressed skiers don't often go to the lodge and warm up, they can easily enter the first stages of hypothermia (a lowering of the body's core temperature by only one to three degrees F). The effects usually involve shivering, a slowing of the reflexes and loss of coordination, all of which are dangerous to a skier. The problem is that most of the symptoms and effects go unnoticed until they are extreme enough to be noticed by fellow skiers. Or they cause the skier to have an accident. I recall one time when a woman skier was helped into a ski lodge with a body temperature of only 91°F: a very dangerous level! She warmed up over several hours, during which time she endured spasms of violent shivering. She recovered without any long-term effects, but in a less controlled environment, the outcome may not have been as favorable.

Hikers, campers and hunters are often unaware of the onset of hypothermia until its effects are quite dangerous. The process is insidious and should be more widely publicized. If the public were more aware of hypothermia's causes and its prevention, there would be fewer victims.

Unfortunately, the media generally call hypothermia "exposure." People don't die from exposure! They die from a lowering of the body's core temperature! The word "exposure" doesn't specify what the victim was exposed to, and it doesn't refer to the *real* problem: lack of proper knowledge and/or preparation. People will become more aware of hypothermia's causes and ways of preventing it only when the media becomes more accurate and specific in its reporting.

One of the most common misconceptions about hypothermia is that it occurs only in below freezing conditions. Wrong! Novice climbers have died from hypothermia while inadequately clothed in 50°F weather. Boaters have been killed by immersion in water 40°F and higher.

Another misconception is hypothermia is a high-altitude problem. There's an increased risk of hypothermia at higher altitudes, but many people have suffered hypothermia at sea level. Moreover, people who travel to higher altitudes are generally more aware of the danger and are better prepared for it.

Each year in this country, there are probably tens of thousands of incidents involving the first stages of hypothermia. Since these episodes aren't fatal, but involve only shivering and discomfort, they're dismissed as harmless. But these incidents are not be as harmless as they first appear. They're setups for disaster which largely went unrecognized as such. Another danger that's generally overlooked is that the body's immune system is depressed in the first stages of hypothermia. A temperature of 95° to 96°F is hard on your body's cells and organs; there are no statistics on the subject, but it's likely that many cases of colds. flu, pneumonia and other sicknesses came about after a "minor" case of hypothermia. The body also suffers some degree of exhaustion while it's recovering from hypothermia; a relatively large amount of glucose is used to fuel the body's cells during hypothermia, and the body takes some time to replenish the stored energy. This temporarily weakens the body and makes it more vulnerable to sickness. (Your mother warned you not to "catch a chill." She was right!)

Predisposing Factors:

Thin or slight build: Fat tissue has greater insulative value than other types of tissue; this is why heavier people tend to feel the cold less than thinner people. Another factor is that a smaller person has a greater ratio of surface area to body volume than a large person; this results in a small person losing body heat faster than a large person. This is great for thin or small runners who have to dispose of body heat which builds up in their muscles, but it's bad for children and smaller/thinner adults who try to stay warm in the winter. It might seem that it would be a good idea to put on a few extra pounds in the winter, but I don't know many people who have such control of their weight that they could quickly shed the extra weight come spring. It's also more efficient to carry your insulation *outside* your skin. You needn't be worried about being thin as long as your insulation is adequate and you keep other factors under control.

Poor cardiovascular condition: This means that your heart, circulatory system and lungs function at reduced efficiency. Therefore, for a given amount of work, you'll expend more effort and tire more quickly; your energy reserves will be lower; and it'll take you longer to recover from fatigue. Almost anyone in poor cardiovascular condition can benefit from the right kind of exercise (under medical supervision, if necessary).

I know of three basic types of exercise: stretching, for flexibility and mobility; strengthening, for building muscles; and cardiovascular, for building endurance and efficiency. Cardiovascular exercises give your heart, lungs and circulatory system a workout. Some of the best exercises of this type are cross-country skiing, bicycling (stationary or moving), swimming, running or jogging, jumping rope and exercise-walking. (The last involves walking fast enough to maintain the elevated heart-rate that's right for you; check this rate with your doctor.)

Cardiovascular exercise makes your heart, lungs and muscles more efficient. Your body can do more with less energy, so you conserve energy which in an emergency might be needed to produce warmth. Not only does it take longer for you to become exhausted, but because of increased cardiovascular efficiency, you'll also recover from exhaustion more rapidly.

Illness: If your body is busy fighting off an illness, it will be in a weakened condition and therefore less efficient in its ability to produce warmth.

Lack of sleep; nervous tension: Either of these can lead to exhaustion.

Causes of Hypothermia:

Lack of proper nutrition or hydration: Either deficiency will cause your body to be unable to produce the energy you need to function effectively and produce the warmth you need. If you become only ten percent dehydrated, your body's ability to control your warmth decreases by approximately thirty-five percent. Adequate food and water are critical for maintaining adequate warmth!

Inadequate clothing: If your clothing isn't *thick* enough or sufficiently windproof/waterproof to maintain your thermal balance, your body will begin to lose heat faster than it can produce it. Your body temperature will start to drop below 98.6°F; this is the beginning of hypothermia.

Getting wet: Overexertion can lead to getting soaked in your own perspiration; this can cause overly rapid cool down which can result in hypothermia. An accidental drenching from falling into a stream can result in rapid cooling from the direct contact with very cold water. A freezing rain can also drench you if your clothing isn't waterproof; the result is a combination of immediate cooling from the rain and subsequent cooling from evaporation of the water in your clothing. To put it simply, water is essential inside your body but is to be totally avoided outside your skin. *Wetness is a grave danger in cold conditions!*

Exhaustion: If you let yourself become exhausted, you're a sitting duck for hypothermia. If the weather turns colder, windier or wetter, your body won't be able to function as well. It won't be able to provide you with more warmth quickly, get you out of the weather faster, or create a needed shelter.

An exhausted state is a weakened one in which the body needs rest and is trying to rebuild its energy. This is the worst time to put additional energy demands on the body. When you get too cold, your body must increase its metabolic rate in organs and muscles to provide the extra warmth you need, but if you're exhausted, the body just can't do it. Then your temperature starts to drop, resulting in hypothermia.

Exhaustion is a condition which isn't really measurable. The old mountain men used to look up at the stars at night to test whether they were too tired to continue to travel safely. If the stars appeared to be still, they knew they weren't exhausted. But if the stars appeared to be swimming a bit, they knew they should stop, make camp and rest; otherwise, they would become exhausted.

Exhaustion can have a number of causes, including insufficient food or water; lack of rest, overexertion with concurrent buildup of lactic acid in the muscles and/or lowering of muscle glycogen; and sudden illness.

To delay the onset of exhaustion during periods of heavy activity, eat snacks frequently, take rest breaks often and pace yourself. Heavy exertion can lead not only to exhaustion, but the rapid breathing that accompanies it results in significant losses of heat and water.

Hikers and climbers sometimes use a technique called rest-step. When going up steep pitches, they don't just plod along step after step, huffing and puffing. In rest-step, a hiker will take one step, rest and take a breath, and only then take another step. If the climber feels that the pulse rate is still too fast, then he or she will take two or three breaths or more between each step. If two steps and then one breath keep the heart rate low enough, then that will be the pace. Whatever it takes to keep your heart rate and respiration rates reasonable is proper pacing.

Injury: The body reacts to injuries in various ways. A serious cut or a broken bone could result in a reduction of the blood flow to the injured area. A serious injury usually is accompanied by shock and a general slowdown of some of the body's systems; there is a marked decrease in the body's ability to stay warm. Hypothermia is a real threat after any injury suffered at any distance from prompt medical attention; in fact, getting injured is one of the leading causes of hypothermia among mountain climbers. An injured person, who's away from the support services of civilization and is in a cold environment, needs every bit of insulation he or she can get. To provide a safety factor in the amount of insulation available to an injured person, groups traveling in the cold should carry sleeping bags appropriate for the coldest temperatures they expect to encounter. Some recommend using lighter sleeping bags and wearing outer clothing in the bag when needed. I disagree with this; your outer clothing should be an extra safety factor.

Preventing Hypothermia

The most important factors within your control to prevent hypothermia are:

- a sufficient thickness of insulation;
- protection from the wind;
- keeping dry (from inside and out);
- proper nutrition and hydration; and
- pacing yourself to prevent fatigue.

It should be noted that increasing the efficiency of your cardiovascular condition takes months, but is worth the effort.

You must have the correct thickness of insulation over enough of your body to balance your heat input with your heat output. (See charts on page 32.) You should wear a windproof outer shell over your insulation, or the wind will negate most of its value. The outer shell should also be waterproof, to prevent rain or snow from getting the insulation wet. Interior moisture can be controlled by using vapor barrier, venting, decreasing insulation as required, slowing the rate of activity, or combining several of these. Consuming enough food and water is important in maintaining your body's ability to produce heat. Finally, you should conserve your energy by pacing yourself; it's crucial to prevent fatigue, which interferes with the body's ability to maintain its warmth.

Recognizing the Symptoms of Hypothermia

Knowing the symptoms and staying alert for them can help avert serious consequences. Early warning can buy the time necessary to take the appropriate steps to keep hypothermia from worsening. Hypothermia is insidious; it creeps up on you. It's harder to spot the symptoms in ourselves than in others. This is one of many reasons it's safer to travel in groups. Following are the symptoms of hypothermia:

Mild Hypothermia:

Body temperature 98° to 96°F: Complaining about feeling cold; shivering starts (for most people, not all) and becomes uncontrollable.

Body temperature below 96°F: Shivering gets worse; speaking becomes difficult; thinking is slower; judgment is affected; memory may seem to fade; stumbling and poor coordination may appear, along with the inability to keep up with a group.

Profound Hypothermia:

Body temperature below 90° F: Muscles show much rigidity; shivering decrease or stops; movements become more erratic; memory may be much worse, with amnesia appearing. But for all those symptoms, the person may still appear to be in contact with surroundings.

Body temperature below 85° F: Person loses contact with surroundings; muscles are still rigid; vital functions are slowed.

Body temperature below 80° F: Unconsciousness usually occurs.

Body temperature below 78° F: Control centers in the brain are affected; cardiac and respiratory functions may be so impaired as to cause death.

Signs to Watch For:

In others: Complaints of feeling cold, stumbling, falling, slurred speech, violent shivering, bad judgment, irrational behavior. People with profound hypothermia may lose urinary control and have fruity acetone breath.

In yourself: Feeling of deep cold, shivering, stumbling, falling, poor coordination.

Tests: Best is to use a special low-reading thermometer. Next best is to try to walk in a straight line for 25 to 30 feet. If you can't, you're probably hypothermic to some degree.

How to Treat Hypothermia in the Field

Mild Hypothermia:

If someone is showing signs of hypothermia, immediate action should be taken. All members of the party should be checked for their condition. All efforts should be made to get the affected person (or persons) out of the elements and to stop the heat loss. If little activity had been undertaken before the hypothermic condition is noticed and if shelter is not too far off, then additional insulation for the hypothermic person and some energetic hiking might be appropriate. However, this is not always the case. Sometimes the victim doesn't have the energy, or suitable shelter is a long way off. The best course of action may be to create a shelter on the spot. If a tent is available, it should be set up.

The victim should be encouraged to do isometric exercises, if possible. All wet clothing should be changed to dry spare clothing from other members of the party. Build a fire, if possible. A curved snow wall in back of the fire can reflect heat forward, as can a Mylar emergency blanket. If a stove is available, it should be used to heat liquids.

If a sleeping bag is available, it should be pre-warmed by another member of the party. Someone in good condition should get into the bag first and strip while inside it, thus generating more warmth. The victim should then have his outer coat removed, be placed in the bag and have the rest of his clothing removed in the bag if possible. The person who warmed the bag should be in the bag naked with the victim to provide needed warmth. More than one other person is better still. (The sleeping bag has no warmth of its own; it's only an insulator. If the victim is placed in the bag without pre-warming it, he or she will continue to lose heat. It's crucial to stop the heat loss.)

The victim should be insulated from the cold ground, by using a waterproof ground cloth plus foam insulation. A sleeping bag alone provides very little protection from conductive heat loss to the ground.

The victim's head and neck area should be well insulated. More than one cap may be useful. If the victim is conscious, his/her mouth should be loosely covered with a layer of wool or synthetic cloth so that inhaled air will be pre-warmed.

NEVER give any alcoholic beverage to someone with hypothermia. If the person is conscious, warm drinks or sweets are OK, but these provide little benefit compared with a warm body in direct contact with the victim. If no sleeping bag is available, other party members can huddle around the victim.

After the victim has recovered somewhat and if conditions allow, he or she should be allowed to continue rewarming for a few hours. When rewarming starts, the victim may feel better after a short time. However, the temperature sensors are in the skin and may fool a person into thinking he or she is warm again when the core temperature is still dangerously low. Once a person has suffered hypothermia, it's probably a good idea to retreat to a civilized setting instead of continuing on a trip. The aftereffects may be exhaustion, and the body will be in a weakened condition for a few days.

Profound Hypothermia:

The victim of profound hypothermia *must be treated very gently: any jarring may cause a fatal arhythmia of the heart.* Profound hypothermia is a grave medical emergency; the victim should be taken to a hospital as soon as possible. The evacuation must be done very gently. The victim of profound hypothermia should not be allowed to move or do anything for himself. Some rescued victims have gotten up, walked a few steps and instantly died on the spot, when cold blood from their extremities hit their heart.

Rapid rewarming should be done in a hospital, if possible. If evacuation to a hospital is impossible, it may be best to slowly rewarm the trunk area only, while preventing further heat loss.

For more information, see: *Hypothermia: Death by Exposure* by William W Forgey, MD and *Hypothermia, Frostbite and Other Cold Injuries;* edited by James A Wilkerson, MD.

FROSTBITE

Like hypothermia, frostbite is a cold-related injury, but it affects individual parts of the body. It acts through actual freezing rather than a lowering of normal temperature. The parts of the body most often affected by frostbite are hands, feet, nose, cheeks, chin and ears.

Predisposing Factors:

Most of the factors involved in hypothermia are also factors creating risk of frostbite: dehydration, lack of rest, inadequate clothing, improper nutrition, poor conditioning, sickness, accident, shock, lack of oxygen, etc.

Anything that impedes blood circulation increases the chances of frostbite. Elastic bands around the wrists or ankles are especially danger-ous even if they don't seem snug; even Velcro closures should not be secured too tightly.

Tight boots cause many cases of frostbite. Avoid adding socks to an already comfortable boot/sock combination. The resulting constriction almost guarantees cold feet and is an invitation to frostbite.

Other Causes and Risks:

Having exposed skin in severe cold is inviting frostbite. Petroleum jelly on the face or hands can be a small help since it reduces the evaporative heat loss from the skin. Below a certain temperature (which varies with individual condition, wind speed, etc.), a face mask and gloves are essential. If in doubt, err on the side of caution. You can always stuff a face mask in your pocket. (Hint for male skiers: Shave at night, not in the morning; you don't want to scrape skin away and open up your pores just before you go into the cold. And even a thin layer of stubble traps a certain amount of air and holds it against your face.)

Walking in deep snow sometimes creates a high risk of frostbite to the feet. If it was well below zero when the snow fell, the temperature of that snow layer will remain extremely cold; this is because snow is an excellent insulator, due to all the air it traps. You may be hiking in +20°F air while your feet are being exposed to temperatures below zero. It pays to have a thermometer with you for a variety of reasons, and this is one of them. If you find that your feet are colder than they should be, don't ignore the situation. Insulate them better or get them out of the snow as soon as possible.

Plastic boots have caused cases of frostbite in the Northwest and Alaska. This is probably due to constriction, since plastic can't expand the way leather does, although it's difficult to think of thick leather mountaineering boots expanding at all. Perhaps the difficulty was too tight a fit without room for expansion. After an hour or so of foot travel, the feet expand. Having boots one size too large is a rule that hikers and climbers should observe.

Mountaineers should take care regarding boot liners. Some of the modern foams, although excellent insulators, can expand at higher elevations (because of reduced air pressure) and cut off circulation to the feet; this may have caused some cases of frostbite.

One of the worst dangers of serious frostbite is the accidental spilling of a highly volatile fluid (such as gasoline for a stove) on your skin. Especially if the gas has cooled down overnight, when it touches bare skin, its own cold and the evaporative heat loss can quickly cool the skin down to -50°F or even -100°F. This almost always causes instantaneous, possibly severe, frostbite; immediate medical attention is required. Filling a stove in extreme cold requires extraordinary caution!

Touching metal with the bare skin in extreme cold can cause frostbite very quickly. At risk are people who are working on cars, adjusting ski bindings or just trying to warm up a key to open a frozen car door lock. If the metal is cold enough, touching it with your bare hand will cause the moisture in the skin to freeze instantly, welding the skin to the metal. When you pull your hand away, skin is ripped away in the process.

Without thinking, someone may automatically pop a cold key in his mouth to warm it up. If the key is cold enough, it will freeze to the tongue. The person panics and grabs it off. This rips some skin from the tongue and is extremely painful. Even if the key were warmed with the hand so it could be removed without ripping the skin, the person would have some frostbitten skin on the tongue. In a word, *never!* is how often you should put a cold key in your mouth.

How Frostbite Acts

When the skin is exposed to extreme cold (whether air, liquid or solid), the blood vessels automatically constrict and reduce blood flow in the area. The smaller arteries will shunt the blood directly to the smaller veins, thus completely bypassing the tiny capillaries which nourish the involved area. Since there is reduced blood flow, there is also reduced heat flow. Liquids in and around the cells will freeze. The longer the cells are in contact with the extreme cold, the worse damage they will sustain. The greatest damage probably is done by:

Intercellular ice crystals which draw additional fluids out of the cells and upset their chemical balance;

The cells being deprived of nutrients and oxygen, plus accumulating waste products; and

Free-radical (chemical) damage after the blood flow is restored.

Types of Frostbite

Frostnip: This is initial pain from the cold, followed by numbness and, after rewarming, a tingling feeling. No real damage occurs. Most people refer to this as frostbite, but that's medically inaccurate. If treated promptly, frostnip will not cause the affected area to be more sensitive to cold, whereas frostbite will. If frostnip is not treated quickly, extensive cell damage will occur, and you will now have real frostbite.

Superficial Frostbite: This involves only the skin and the tissue not far beneath the skin. The affected area will be white and frozen to the touch, but the tissue beneath it will be soft and resilient. This can be determined by pressing gently yet firmly to feel the layer under the frozen area, and before any rewarming has taken place. After rewarming, time will tell how deep the damage is. In a light case of superficial frostbite, the area will become numb after rewarming, then turn a dark mottled color and start to sting and burn for an extended time. In worse cases, blisters will form after 24 to 36 hours, and the pain of the injury may last several weeks. Even after the pain subsides, the injured area will be very tender for a while and very sensitive to any cold, possibly for years.

Deep Frostbite: This also involves deeper tissue, possibly through the bone, and is more serious. Before rewarming, the injured area will be hard as a board. Blisters usually will form in three to seven days, and will be larger than in superficial frostbite. There will be a greater amount of swelling, which may last many weeks. Pain may be great and last many weeks. The damaged tissue discolors profoundly and finally sloughs off, leaving an ultra-sensitive area which may take many months to heal. The body seems to be much better than a surgeon in separating the dead tissue from the healing tissue. When surgery is performed to remove dead tissue, more tissue loss often occurs than would have occurred without surgery. The modern method is to let the body heal by itself, while preventing infection. A year or more in a hospital bed is worth the wait if you get to keep your limbs. Even if surgery is needed to relieve pressure from profound swelling, or for severe gangrene, make sure the doctor treating you or yours is aware of the most modern methods of frostbite treatment.

Prevention

Almost all of the preventive measures listed under "Hypothermia" are appropriate for frostbite.

Don't wear tight-fitting shoes or boots; also, no tight bands at wrists and ankles.

If the weather doesn't seem cold enough for a face mask, put petroleum jelly or skin cream on the face.

Use the buddy system if you're traveling with others; observe each other for facial white splotches that signify the beginning of frostbite. Stop! Warm the affected area before moving on. Don't wait until you have a real case of frostbite.

If your feet are extremely cold and painful, or if they get numb after being very cold, *stop!* Don't continue traveling under these conditions unless your life is at stake (say, from hypothermia or pulmonary edema). Make camp, or get out of the weather long enough to rewarm your feet. If shelter isn't available, putting your feet against someone else's bare stomach is a common, effective usual method of rewarming them. (You need good friends for this!) Otherwise cup them in your own hands or tuck them under your coat as you sit.

Wear thin liner-gloves under your gloves or mittens. They will allow you to do a certain amount of work in cold conditions while still giving you a lot of manual dexterity. Stop and rewarm your hands when necessary.

Treatment

Frostnip can be treated in the field, as noted above. If your face is involved, you can rewarm it by placing your hands against the area until it's warm again. If your hands are involved, put them in your parka under your armpits, or against someone else's warm skin. Never try to rewarm an area of skin by rubbing, and especially never by rubbing snow against the affected area. This is an old wive's tale and can only worsen the injury.

Real frostbite calls for evacuation and medical attention as soon as possible. If evacuation to a hospital cannot be accomplished immediately, the injured person should be helped to a low camp as soon as possible. The victim should then be given shelter, food, adequate insulation and rest. Instead of stopping, it's better for the victim to walk, even on frozen feet, for a few hours if a better, warmer camp can be created at a lower elevation. Once the frozen area is rewarmed, it's subject to even worse consequences if it gets refrozen. (Refreezing usually means much more tissue loss and even loss of limbs that otherwise could have been saved.) There are many cases of people walking for days with completely frozen legs and feet and having no loss of limbs, just some lost toes. This result was achieved because they were able to get to medical facilities before their frozen limbs were rewarmed.

Some DON'TS for the field:
- Don't let the victim have any tobacco or alcohol.
- Don't try to walk on thawed feet.
- Don't break blisters.
- Don't rub or scrub the affected areas.
- Don't remove any tissue; nature will do that, if necessary.
- Don't rewarm with extreme heat or very dry heat; additional injury might result.

The appropriate treatment for frostbite, either superficial or deep, is to have the affected areas rewarmed rapidly in a 110°F waterbath (never above 114°F). Continue rewarming until the affected area losses its paleness: usually no more than about twenty minutes. This process usually is painful and requires medication. Aspirin is recommended for pain and for its action in the frostbitten area. Shock is also a risk for a frostbitten person entering a warmer environment. Rapid rewarming should not be tried in the field unless continued warmth can be assured and imminent medical attention can be relied on. Hospital care is needed to provide aseptic treatment, to prevent further injury, to care for shock and pain, and to give the patient general health care during recovery. The process of recovering for deep frostbite may take many months, even a year or more.

IMPORTANT!: Doctors now have access to drugs (some only experimental) for use in preventing tissue damage in cases of short-term heart or circulatory stoppage. It seems that considerable damage is caused by free-radical chemicals that form when circulation is resumed. It's possible that some of the damage from frostbite may be due to the same cause. If this is the case, then much tissue damage may be prevented by giving large amounts of anti-oxidants (these are chemicals that render free-radicals harmless) to frostbite victims before rewarming is started and afterwards as well. One of the well-known anti-oxidants in Europe is Hydergine, made by the Sandoz Company. Other anti-oxidants are: BHT, vitamin C, vitamin E, zinc, selenium and some of the B vitamins.

For more information on anti-oxidants, see the book *Life Extension* by Durk Pearson and Sandy Shaw. For more information on frostbite, see *Frostbite* by Bradford Washburn, a publication of the Museum of Science, Boston; *Hypothermia: Death by Exposure* by William W Forgey, MD; and *Hypothermia, Frostbite and Other Cold Injuries*, edited by James A Wilkerson, MD.

IMMERSION FOOT

This is commonly known as trench foot. It is an injury similar to frostbite in the damage it can cause and also in its localized effect. It is unlike frostbite in that it doesn't require freezing temperatures but can cause damage even at temperatures even above 60°F. It usually occurs when the feet remain cold and damp for long periods, such as when soldiers have to stand in, or march through, wet trenches; hence the name.

When the feet are subjected to cool or cold temperatures, the body responds by shutting down circulation, first to the skin in that area and then to the tissue just under the skin. If the condition persists a long time, the lack of blood supply (with its load of nutrients, oxygen and *heat*) will kill some tissue and damage other tissue in the area.

Symptoms include cold, swollen feet; dark splotches on the feet; tissue that's waxy and resilient (as compared with hard and frozen when frostbitten); and loss of feeling. Treatment in the field should include drying the feet, warming them and taking aspirin to help prevent blood-clots. A victim of trench foot should seek medical treatment as soon as possible, because gangrene may be one of the aftereffects. Obviously, prevention is important. Make sure you do everything possible to maintain warmth for your feet. Never wear anything tight-fitting on the feet; the constriction of blood circulation can help cause frostbite or immersion foot. Keep feet dry by changing socks frequently. Dry and massage the feet to help the circulation.

Vapor barrier for the feet is one way to prevent cold injury, but if it is used incorrectly, it may be inviting trench foot. Incorrect use includes either too tight a fit, which constricts blood vessels, or insufficient insulation on top of the vapor barrier, which actually could cause the condition you're trying to avoid: cold, wet feet. When used correctly, vapor barrier can't be beat for efficiency. The "Mickey Mouse" boots used by the Army in Korea are vapor barrier boots; they keep the feet warm (although sometimes wet) in very cold conditions. Mountaineers use vapor barrier in extreme cold conditions; they find that it really helps prevent frostbite.

IMMERSION HYPOTHERMIA

One of the greatest dangers of hypothermia is immersion in cool or cold water. Since the density of water is much greater than air, direct contact with water causes heat loss from the body at a rate 240 times faster than contact with the air. Anyone who is involved with boating, whether commercially or for pleasure, should be aware of the dangers of immersion hypothermia. Even in warm weather, it is extremely dangerous to be immersed in cool water for a lengthy period.

There are three ways immersion in cold water can kill:

Arctic waters, or any body of water around 32°F, can kill by cold shock in a matter of seconds. Shock to the heart or loss of breathing control causes drowning.

Cold water numbs muscles within minutes and can cause an otherwise strong swimmer to drown. The cold also causes the body to reduce blood flow to the extremities, and the muscles don't get the nutrients and oxygen they need to work. What looks like a short swim in cold water can so fatigue the muscles that drowning occurs.

Cold water can conduct heat away from your body very quickly, leading to hypothermia and death. Average survival time in freezing waters (32°F) is from thirty seconds to three minutes. A Coast Guard chart lists the possibilities for survival in water: at 40°F, survival time is about twenty minutes; at 50°F, it's about one hour; for 60°F, it's two hours. It's important to know the temperature of the water in your area so that you can gauge the danger and prepare appropriately.

Survival times vary with differences in physical makeup. People with more subcutaneous fat will tend to have a longer survival time because of the insulating value of the fat. The more clothing you have on, the longer your survival time is likely to be. Another important point is that exercise speeds up heat loss in the water. Unless your swim to safety is very short and you're sure you can make it, you're better off just staying still, holding on and waiting for help. Isometric exercises, which don't move your body in the water, will help.

Closed-cell foam is the best insulation when immersed in water. It is also the best insulation for life jackets and survival suits. Dry survival suits, which don't allow water to enter at the cuffs or ankles, are better than wet suits. The thicker they are, the better. Full body suits are far better than partial suits. Some of the best survival suits include: ILC Industries Prototype Survival Suit, Bayley Exposure Suit, SIDEP Seastep Survival Suit and Helly-Hanson Survival Suit.

If recreational boaters don't want this level of protection, at least they should get life jackets that provide thick closed-cell foam, protect the head, have arms and are lined with nylon for ease in donning. Foam pants should also be carried. This combination is like a wet suit; it doesn't provide the degree of protection of dry survival suits, but it's much more protection than just an armless life jacket.

To show how little protection a life jacket provides, consider just one incident at sea. In December 1963, the *Lakonia* caught fire. The water temperature was relatively warm (64°F). Rescue vessels were on the scene within three hours, but 113 people were found floating dead in their life jackets. In the past, this type of death was listed only as drowning. It is only recently that authorities and the press have begun to learn that the real cause is drowning *due to hypothermia.*

Because of the survival suits, a better example is being set today. There has been an increase in the number of incidents involving people who were found alive and well after 24 hours in cold water because they were able to don a survival suit before entering the water. Some are fishermen, who started wearing the suits as a matter of course in cold conditions. A sadder note is the case in which a sailor's companions ridiculed him for putting on his suit at the first sign that their boat was in trouble. The vessel sank, and out of thirty men, the "cautious" sailor was the only survivor.

SURVIVAL AT SEA

Survival at sea in a lifeboat may depend more on staying warm than on having a supply of food or water. Strong winds and regular dousings by the ocean or rain can quickly sap the strength of anyone not well protected from the elements. Death from hypothermia can result in only a few hours under these conditions. The 1986 Coast Guard standards for lifeboats on commercial vessels call for a completely covered craft (hard-cover). This is a long overdue change. The requirements for pleasure vessels also calls for complete cover, but only part of the cover has to be hard-cover.

Preparation: For lifeboat survival gear to be effective in cold conditions, it should include, in addition to the regular survival gear, special cold weather clothing specifically designed for wet weather conditions (especially if the lifeboats don't have a complete cover). When you're in a lifeboat, struggling against wind-driven rain, waves and water, regular rain gear won't keep you dry or warm. Closed-cell foam is the best insulation for these conditions. Lifevests should be made of this foam. Neoprene rubber is a closed-cell foam that is used in cold weather diving suits. It's a good insulator, but rather heavy. Other closed-cell foams such as *Ensolite* and *Ethafoam* are excellent insulators and much lighter than neoprene. Neoprene is stronger than the lighter, warmer foams and can be used as an outer layer to protect the weaker foams. Strong nylon outerwear can also protect the other foams.

A well-stocked lifeboat should provide adequate full body insulation for all the persons it's designed to carry. This means protection for the head, hands, feet and legs, as well as the trunk. Vapor barrier suits (of polyethylene or some other plastic) should be stocked if a sufficient amount of foam insulation isn't available.

What to do: If you're caught in a lifeboat in cold conditions, check the provisions. If vapor barrier is available, wear it on top of your underwear and put your other clothes back on top of it. Try to cover your head and neck. If you were wet when you got into the lifeboat, try to change into dry clothing. At the least, take off the wet clothes and wring them out so that they are as dry as possible before you put them on again. If rain gear is available, wear it even over wet clothes (after wringing) so that the evaporative cooling rate is slowed. If water evaporates too quickly from your clothes, you can become hypothermic. Isometric exercise should be done to maintain body heat while the clothes are drying or any time more body heat is required. It's important to do isometric exercises when shivering starts; they're more efficient than shivering. People should also huddle together for warmth. If you have large jackets or overcoats, these should be placed on top of more than one person, rather than in between persons. Put your arms inside your outerwear and against your body. Tuck your legs into your chest to conserve body heat.

EMERGENCY SHELTERS

Any time you're in extreme weather conditions you're not prepared to withstand, *seek shelter with haste!* Many who tried to bull their way through are now only mute statistics, demonstrating that the forces of nature must be respected. You can coexist with nature, but it's a fool's game to try to beat nature.

The key here is knowing how to recognize when you are in an emergency situation. This knowledge can come from what you've read, what you've learned by experience or even from your intuition. If the time comes when you realize that your clothing is insufficient for the existing conditions, you should acknowledge an emergency and take stock of your situation. If both advancing and retreating are ill-advised (or would mean further loss of body heat), it's time to seek shelter.

Time is the other key. The real basis of this book is energy conservation! *Temperature, wind and water are acting in concert with time to rob you of your body heat.* Your job is disrupt this combination. You must find shelter, and you must do so quickly. If you delay, your hands may get too numb to build a shelter. Also, if you wait too long, your body may cool down to a point where the shelter you create is insufficient for your *new* need for rewarming.

Let's say you get caught in a storm at –10°F in a strong wind. As quickly as possible, you dig a snow cave. After you're in the cave, the inside temperature rises until it's about 35 to 45 degrees higher than the outside temperature, and there is no wind. You're warm from building the cave, and you have to remove an outer layer of clothing to cool off for a while. (You'd better have some closed-cell foam to keep you warm and dry while sitting in the snow.) Now that you are out of the weather, your clothing is probably good enough to protect you for for days, if necessary.

A second scenario for the same conditions would have you struggle on until you're exhausted before you give up trying to get somewhere on foot. You're lucky if you still have the dexterity to dig a cave, but even if you do, your body has cooled down to below 98.6°F. *Remember: It takes far less energy to stay warm than to rewarm.* Since you're exhausted, you don't have much energy left for rewarming. It might take hours of isometric exercises to rewarm, and you may not have enough energy left to continue exercising. Waiting until you are too tired to go on can leave you in *deep trouble.*

What is a Shelter?

When you're in an emergency situation and your life and limbs, or those of someone in your party, are threatened by the elements (*cold, wind and water, acting over time*); anything that will separate you from the elements is a shelter. This means *anything!* It could be a phone booth, an abandoned mine, a car, a house, a cardboard box, a lean-to, a hole in the snow, or a wall of rocks. Some of these may shelter you from wind and water but not the cold. This is better than no shelter at all, since the combination of the elements is much worse than just the cold alone. Anything you can find or build can serve as a shelter. Even if you have to break into a building illegally, it would be absurd not to do so if your life is at stake.

Shelters You Can Build

Even if you're away from civilization, building blocks for a shelter are all around you. In a wooded area, tree limbs, branches and leaves can be used. Above timberline, every rock and pebble is a potential building block for a wall to protect you from the wind. If you get into trouble in snow country, you should know that snow is a good insulator as well as a great building material.

Wooded areas have many potential shelters. A hollow next to a large tree can become a shelter by putting branches or pine boughs over it. A large downed tree can also be used. Place branches against the tree and cover them with more branches, leaves, plastic, twigs, brush, dirt: *anything* to create a roof. Try to close at least one end of the shelter, so that it will trap heat.

A lean-to is constructed by putting a log across the branches of two trees four to six feet apart. The log should be placed three to five feet high, with lots of branches placed against it (as in the previous example). If only one side is covered, you'll have a roof overhead, but it won't protect you from wind or driven rain as much as a multi-sided lean-to. By enclosing the area almost completely and covering it with boughs and leaves, you'll have a shelter that can retain some of your body heat.

A sheath knife or small hatchet are useful in building shelters, but a small folding saw is even better. The saw on Swiss Army knives is also excellent. Some camping stores sell a survival saw, whose cutting edge is like miniature barbed wire. It's great for cutting even branches that are three to four inches thick; it's inexpensive and weighs only about an ounce. The type that comes with rings at both ends can even be made into a bow saw with just one branch, so that you can use it with one hand.

SNOW SHELTERS

Snow is a good insulator because it contains a lot of air, and if it has the right consistency, it makes good building blocks. Fresh snow can sometimes be light and easy to work with.

Four types of snow shelters are described here: **snow trench, snow cave, igloo and quin-zhee hut.** Various combinations of these shelters are also possible.

The most important shelter to learn about is the **snow trench** because it's the quickest and easiest to build and can be built just about anywhere in almost any type of snow.

Since various snow conditions exist in different areas or even in the same area at different times of the day, it helps to know which snow shelters are appropriate for which type of snow. As noted, the snow trench can be built in just about any type of snow. The snow cave is next in degree of difficulty, and it can be created in many different snow conditions. The igloo is feasible when the snow is compressed enough that it can be cut into blocks. Wind-driven snow has a hard surface and is good for igloos. Sticky snow that packs well is also good for igloos. Loose, dry snow that looks unusable for construction is, in fact, perfect for quin-zhee huts, as long as there's a difference in temperature between the top and bottom of the snow pack.

Snow Trench

This type of shelter is an absolute "must-know" for anyone traveling away from civilization in snow country. It's the easiest to learn and usually the easiest and fastest to build, and it can be built in almost any type of snow. There's a double irony in using a snow trench in an emergency. First, you use snow to protect you from the cold; second, you dig a pit that looks like a grave in order to save your life.

How to build: Simply dig a hole in the snow that is six feet long by three feet wide by two feet deep. (See page 138.) A shovel is a good tool to use, but anything can be used in an emergency; even a packframe with an empty pack or a cup or your hands will do in an emergency. The dimensions don't have to be exact, but leave enough room at the sides and at each end so that your body doesn't touch the snow. As with any snow shelter, your back should be protected with a closed-cell foam pad

SNOW TRENCH

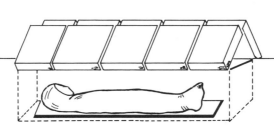

Dig out a trench in the snow about 6′ × 3′ and 2′ deep. If you can cut snow blocks, lean them against each other to form a roof over the trench. Seal off one end this way also. Fill cracks between the blocks with snow. Seal off other end with a block or your pack.

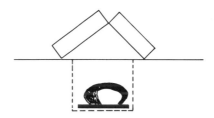

Make sure to put your foam pad and sleeping bag (and ground cloth) down before you build the roof. Allow a small air hole to remain in the roof near the foot and the head. Keep your shovel inside with you.

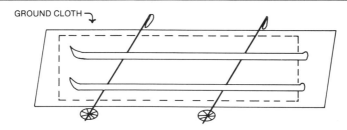

GROUND CLOTH

If the snow can't be made into blocks, use skis & poles, branches, packs, or anything else that will help create a cover for the trench. Cover this with a ground cloth, pack snow on the edges of the ground cloth outside the trench and try to get some loose snow cover on the top if possible.

to keep you warm and dry. A plastic ground cloth will help keep your clothing or sleeping bag dry. A sleeping bag is desirable, but with enough clothing, you can survive without it. Lack of a sleeping bag may necessitate lots of isometric exercise and not allow for much sleep.

To put a top on the trench, cut snow blocks and lean them against each other to form a V-shaped roof; for maximum efficiency, the snow blocks should be cut from the area of the trench itself. Add snow between the cracks in the blocks to seal up your mini-cave. If the trench is strong enough, add loose snow on top for extra warmth. Use skis, pack or anything available to seal off the end you climb into. Be sure to leave a small air hole. Make sure you take some kind of tool inside with you in case you have to dig your way out through packed snow in the morning.

If the snow doesn't pack well enough to form blocks for the roof, try stomping down a small area of snow (about ten feet square), give it a little time to consolidate and try again to cut blocks. If this doesn't work, forget the blocks and use your skis, poles, branches, pack, etc., together with a groundcloth to cover the trench. If the top of the trench will hold it, add snow on top to provide insulation.

If there isn't enough snow-cover to dig down far enough, then dig to ground level and build up walls around the trench. If the snow packs well, you can cut blocks for the walls. If the snow is too loose, just shovel it to your walls and pack it slightly. Then build a roof as described above.

Snow Cave

Anywhere the snowpack is sufficiently deep, you can probably build a snow cave. The snow should be consolidated enough so that it doesn't collapse as you dig. Sometimes a steep area will have plenty of snow at the bottom, even if it's just the steep face of a boulder. Dig into the side of a snow mound rather than into the front, where the snow deposits. Also, be careful not to dig in at the bottom of an avalanche slope.

If the snow is the right consistency, the best way to dig a cave is to cut blocks and remove them. The best tool for a snow cave is a snow saw or a pruning saw (or machete, bayonet, etc.). Next best is a shovel. Or use anything that will work.

How to build: Start low on the snow drift and dig a hole straight in about three feet in diameter. (See page 140.) Turn up at about a 45-degree angle for another three feet, and then dig straight in again and start enlarging the area in front of you. Angling up at 45 degrees before you dig inward will make your sleeping platform higher than the air inlet, so you'll be in the higher, warmer air.) Dig out enough to make a shelf for your waterproof groundcloth, foam pad and sleeping bag. If necessary, you can create a wide enough area for two or more people.

SNOW CAVE

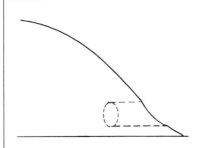

1) Start digging low into the snow bank. Dig a 2½ to 3 foot diameter tunnel into the snow.

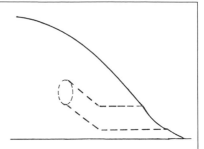

2) After digging inward about 3', start going up at a 45° incline.

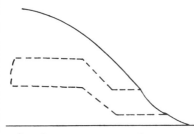

3) When you get to an elevation just above the top of the entrance height, start going straight in again, and also dig out to the sides.

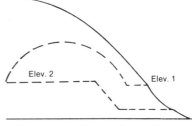

4) Carve a dome shape above for strength and smooth it as much as possible to prevent dripping. (Elev. 1 should be lower than Elev.2).

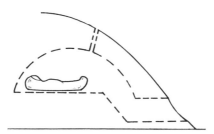

5) Make a small hole in the roof with ski pole, stick, or saw for air. Close entrance with pack or THIN layer of snow.

Form an inner dome by carving the snow overhead; this will give the cave needed strength. Smooth the overhead snow dome as well as you can to prevent dripping. Make a hole in the roof with a stick or ski pole for ventilation. If you intend to use a stove or make a small fire, create the vent hole right above where the stove or fire will be. The vent should be about two inches wide; in use, it will widen by melting some of the snow around it. Make sure the opening at the cave entrance is large enough to admit sufficient air for the cave occupant(s) and the fire. You can carve a few small shelves for items you want to keep handy.

The smaller the snow cave, the warmer it will be. Larger caves with interconnecting chambers are for fun times. Caves just large enough to hold its occupants huddled together are the most appropriate for emergencies.

Quin-Zhee Hut

This is another type of snow cave. The Athapaskan Indians in northern Canada taught travelers how to built it. This shelter can be constructed when the snow is too loose for a cave or igloo blocks, or when the snow cover is only one to three feet thick. A quin-zhee hut requires a temperature difference between the surface snow and the snow near the ground. Mixing snows of differing temperatures causes the snow to harden; this process is called sintering and is sometimes used to build temporary roads in the far north.

How to build: Building a quin-zhee hut is more work than burrowing into an existing snow bank. First you must shovel all the snow you need into a large mound; this can take many hours. Then you have to wait one to three hours for it to harden; only after that can you hollow out the cave.

For one or two persons, you'll want an interior at least five feet in diameter. Add two feet for the thickness of the walls (one foot for each side) at the bottom dimension, and you have an outside diameter of seven feet. To start, mark in the snow a circle seven or eight feet in diameter. Inside this circle, mix the snow near the ground with the snow above it. A shovel is best for this operation, but use anything you have to do the job. A snowshoe works great as a shovel; a ski can be used; a packframe with an empty pack will work. Be inventive!

After the snow within the circle is mixed, add snow to it from outside the circle. Alternate layers of top snow and bottom snow so that you get a mix of snow temperatures. You don't have to mix this snow since it's being applied in layers of different temperatures. When the mound is about six or seven feet high, it should be big enough for a cave.

Don't pack down the snow. Just flatten the top slightly to give it a dome shape; this shape gives it strength. Now you have to wait one to three hours for the sintering process to harden the snow pile into a mass solid enough for you to hollow out. The colder it is outside, the faster this process takes place. If it's about –30°F, then an hour and a half probably will do it. Temperatures below zero are particularly good for building a quin-zhee hut.

While the snow mound is hardening, if the conditions permit, you can build a small fire nearby, cook some food or keep warm by doing isometric exercises. When the snow is sufficiently hard that it won't crumble, start hollowing out the cave. Dig a small opening at ground level (try to keep it small) and continue to dig to the center of the pile. Scoop out the interior snow to form a domed circle. Leave the roof at least fifteen inches thick for strength. To check out the roof's thickness, poke a thin stick or ski pole through it and go out and mark it. Now go back inside and pull it back in, first holding your hand on it against the roof to mark the inside. When you pull it back in, the distance between your hand and the mark you made outside is the thickness of the roof. If the roof is too thin, add snow to the top a bit at a time. Don't try to pack it down or it might cave in! Let it compact by itself, over time.

Continue to hollow out the sides of the cave and clear the snow all the way down to the ground, because that will probably be the warmest surface. Poke a small air hole through the top of the cave; it should be about a half-inch to an inch wide. Another hole is needed lower down to allow air in, unless your doorway isn't completely closed. For a door, you can use a pack or a large rock or loose snow. If you use snow, make the door thin, leave a small air hole and be prepared to chop it away in the morning because it will harden. It's best to leave a opening just large enough for you to crawl through and not bother with a door.

Just as in the igloo and snow cave, the ceiling can be smoothed so that it won't drip on you. Add snow to any outside area that may seem too thin. Scoop out a shelf or two if you need them. If you have a candle, you can use a spoon as a shelf by inserting the spoon into the wall with its bowl sticking out to hold the candle. A gas stove requires a small vent (two to three inches) directly above it. Too small a vent will allow carbon monoxide to build up.

Igloo

Long before Buckminster Fuller gave us the modern geodesic dome, the natives of the far north were building snow domes, known to us as igloos.

The igloo is an excellent structure, fun to know about and often crucial for survival. Its construction requires a little more skill and work than are necessary for building a snow cave, but it's definitely a shelter worth knowing about. Since its snow blocks are not compressed, the igloo may be a bit warmer than a snow cave (the blocks hold more dead air). The roof vent can also be a bit smaller (about ¾-inch), because there's a lot of air in the blocks. The snow blocks also soak up a lot of vapor before they become glazed, so the ceiling probably won't drip as readily as in a snow cave. A well built igloo is strong and warm, and it can last for years in the far north. Even in moderate climates, it is non-polluting and leaves no trace in the spring. Moreover, the igloo you build for fun could save the next traveler's life.

The best tool for igloo building is a snow saw, but a pruning saw will do just as well, or a machete or even a shovel. In a real pinch, even a ski or pole or your hands (with waterproof mittens) can be used. An igloo that looks like a lopsided mess is warmer than no igloo.

A real snow saw is usually made of aluminum; it's about ³⁄₃₂-inch thick, eighteen inches long and weighs only six to eight ounces. It should be carried by any party of three or more and could be taken even by solo travelers. A shovel is a *must* for any size party; actually, each person should have a shovel, in case the group has to break up.

The best snow for an igloo is wind-blown and somewhat compressible. It should not be ice or even very compacted snow. If the snow doesn't hold together when cut into blocks, try compressing the snow with snowshoes or skis. If it doesn't hold together after this, change plans and build a quin-zhee hut.

There's more than one way to build an igloo. Probably the easiest is the double spiral (even if it sounds complicated). Without a spiral, the blocks tend to fall when they're shaped to tilt inward to form the dome shape. A spiral allows the previously placed block to make side contact with the newly placed block, thus holding it from falling in. A double spiral gives a steeper pitch and better contact with the side of the previous block. A dome is the strongest shape and also the warmest. It has the least surface area for the most interior volume; less surface area means less area for heat to escape.

How To Build:

Start by laying out a circle in the snow. (See page 144.) An inside diameter of five feet is sufficient for two people in an emergency. A larger diameter, up to nine feet, is more comfortable for a longer stay or for more people. An igloo with an interior diameter greater than nine feet is more difficult to construct unless you're really experienced.

Cut the first three or four blocks (each about eighteen inches long, twelve inches high and ten to twelve inches thick) out of the snow inside the circle; skip one foot at the circumference and cut four more blocks outside the circle. These will be part of the tunnel entrance. You can cut

THE IGLOO

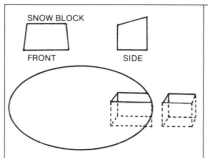

1) Draw a 6' circle in the snow. Cut the first few blocks from inside the circle, then skip a foot and cut a few more. This will later be part of your tunnel entrance.

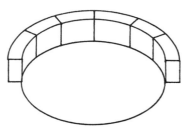

2) Cut blocks and place them in a semicircle.

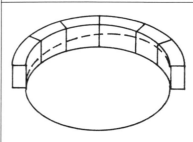

3) Mark a diagonal line from the top of the first block to the bottom of the last block in the semicircle.

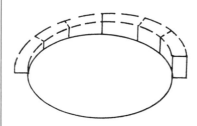

4) Cut the blocks down along this marked line. Now repeat steps 2 and 3 for the second half of the circle. Put large side of first block of first half circle against small side block in second half.

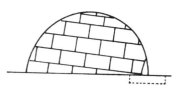

5) Cut out snow blocks from surrounding area. Start adding full blocks to the semi-circles from low sides up. After topping off, cut hole for entrance.

6) Add small tunnel to entrance if time and weather allow. Fill all cracks and thin spots with snow. Poke an air hole in roof. Seal entrance with THIN layer of snow; with an air hole here, too.

out the door itself when you are almost finished. Face the entrance across the prevailing wind, not into it.

Place the first course of blocks in one complete circle.

Make a mark at any point on this course; directly opposite this, make another mark. Around the course of blocks, draw a line connecting the top of the first mark with the bottom of the second mark; this will be a diagonal line on half of the first course. Repeat the process for the other half. Trim the tops of the first course blocks down to the diagonal lines. When you have completed this tapering, you will have the beginnings of two spirals.

Lay new blocks against the exposed surfaces of the last blocks laid. Make sure the blocks are tilted slightly inward to form the dome shape. Some experimenting will be necessary here.

After each course of blocks, use snow to fill any gaps. This prevents drafts and increases the strength of the dome.

Continue until the spirals close in on themselves on the last two blocks. If the dome shape isn't perfect, don't worry about it; a poorly constructed shelter is better than no shelter. Close the top as best you can. You may want to put skis, snowshoes or branches on top and then add more snow to close it and make it wind tight. A little second effort at topping off the igloo should work if the first effort isn't perfect.

Cut an arched hole in the side of the dome where you cut your first blocks. This doorway should be only large enough to allow you just to crawl in; too large an opening will allow cold air to enter and warm air to escape. You can put a thin block of snow in the doorway to stay warmer. Make sure you take your cutting tools inside with you; you may find them useful when you want to get out.

Cut blocks to form a tunnel over the trench outside the entrance to protect yourself better from the wind and to make the igloo slightly warmer. (This is not a necessity).

Poke a small (¾ inch) hole in the ceiling for air.

Complete by smoothing the ceiling so that it won't drip if the interior of the igloo gets too warm. Add snow around the outside where the night wind will be coming from; this strengthens the dome and protects it against erosion. Inspect the dome from the inside; thin areas will show up as light spots. Increase their thickness by adding snow to the exterior. Any new snow that falls on the dome will make it warmer and eventually strengthen it.

As with other snow shelters, waterproof clothing or a waterproof ground cloth are essential for protection against getting soaked by the snow. A foam pad to lie on also is a must.

Don't let the inside of the igloo get too warm or it might weaken the structure. Enlarge the roof vent hole slightly if necessary. If you're going to use a stove or have a *small* fire inside the igloo, make another vent (two to three inches wide) directly above it. This hole probably will become larger from the heat. It's easy to get temperatures from 30°F to 38°F inside an igloo just from your body heat. Some people have trouble sleeping in igloos because their winter sleeping bags are too warm for above-zero temperatures.

How to Build Fires

If you plan well and know how to dress properly for cold weather, you should never have to build a fire. Murphy's Law (*If anything can go wrong, it will!*) unfortunately is always at work, especially when we're away from the comforts of home. Therefore, you should know how to build a fire.

Fire-Making Materials

When you travel away from the conveniences of civilization, your emergency equipment should include matches and/or a lighter, as well as some tinder or a tube of commercial fire-gel, solid-fuel tablets or a candle. Some camping stores also sell a flint stick (or Metal Match) which can be struck with a knife to produce a spark necessary to ignite the tinder. They also sell windproof, waterproof matches which come in handy in rough weather. Probably the easiest way to go is to use a lighter and fire-gel (such as Mautz Fire Ribbon).

If you don't have any tinder, find some dry bark (cedar or birch are excellent) and pound it a bit to powder it. Another possibility is use a knife to shave some very small pieces of a dead branch. Dry weeds will also work, as will pine sap and material in the sheltered areas of pines and spruce.

Next gather several handfuls of kindling wood, such as twigs or small dead branches about the thickness of a pencil. This so-called "squaw wood" should snap easily, or it's too green for kindling. The kindling serves to expand the small fire started in the tinder and keep it going long enough to ignite larger pieces of fuel.

Gather as much wood as you expect to need to keep the fire going for a few hours. Obviously, you should try to find dead branches. If that's not possible, you can use shrubs, dead roots or any material that will burn.

What to Do

One of the easiest methods of starting a fire is to place tinder at the center of a teepee-arrangement of kindling. Leave room between the two by leaning pieces of kindling against each other and not on the tinder.

Leave a small space in the kindling toward the wind so it can fan the flame a bit to get it started. Light the tinder and, if necessary, gently blow on it so the flame will catch. Make sure you blow on it from the side so you don't get smoke in your face. After the tinder ignites the kindling, add some more kindling and then put on the larger wood. Keep the fire small, so that you can control it and make your firewood last longer.

Another way to build a fire is to push a stick into the ground at an angle and pile tinder under it and kindling around or on top of it. Still another way is to pile tinder next to a rock or large dead branch and place kindling against it. Clearly, there are many ways to arrange materials for a fire. The key point is first to get the tinder burning and then have the kindling close enough that it ignites easily but not so close that it smothers the tinder fire.

If you're using a "Metal Match," scrape a knife blade on it toward the tinder to cause a spark to ignite the tinder. Blow on it gently, if needed, to help it flame. If you don't have a match or lighter and if the sun is shining, you can use a magnifying glass (or the lens from a telescope or binoculars) to focus the sun's rays on the tinder and ignite it.

Try to locate your fire near large rocks, leaving enough room so that you can sit comfortably between the fire and the rocks. The rocks will reflect the fire's heat back on you, and you won't have one frozen side.

In Deep Snow

Obviously, you should avoid building a fire under snow-laden branches (remember the old Jack London story?). Stomp out a platform in the snow with your skis, snowshoes or shovel. Place some larger logs together as a platform for the fire, or it will sink quickly into the snow. If it's an emergency (the only reason you should be making a fire in the first place!), cut down a tree, if necessary, to provide a platform of green wood which will last longer before it starts to burn. If you are stranded for any length of time, the platform will slowly sink and can be rebuilt nearby.

EPILOGUE

It's pleasant to end a book on a happy note, especially when that ending also teaches an important lesson. In this case, the lesson is that it's desirable, sometimes crucial, to carry and know how to use equipment suitable for the worst anticipated conditions. But in survival situations, it's even more important — *much more important!* — to make maximum use of any and all available equipment (even if it seems inadequate) and to use calm, reasoned intelligence in employing survival techniques such as those detailed in this book.

A clear demonstration of how this can save lives occurred on Mount Hood in May 1992, six years almost to the day after seven teenage students and two teachers perished after a sudden blizzard hit the 11,235-foot Oregon peak on May 12, 1986. Unlike the conditions in 1986, the morning weather on Mount Hood this Saturday was clear and warm: a beautiful spring day. Six climbers (all in their thirties) began what they expected to be the relatively easy one-day climb to Mount Hood's summit and back. They reached the summit by noon. So far, so good: all expectations realized. But as the six began their descent, the weather on the mountain suddenly turned frighteningly severe. Quickly the peak was engulfed by fog and blowing, blinding snow; as the blizzard settled in, winds exceeded 60 mph and the wind-chill plummeted to –40°F.

Above timberline, where there are no trees to slow the whipping winds, the six climbers inched down the suddenly slippery rocks and snowfields. At the 9,500-foot level, below the crevassed area, they untied from their climbing ropes. One team of three, led by a man with a fair amount of mountaineering experience, purposely slid down one side of a ridge into a canyon area; they quickly realized they were off the normal route and signaled the other team not to follow. That second team proceeded down the other side of the ridge and succeeded in reaching Timberline Lodge at 5,900 feet a few hours later.

The team in the canyon carried a little high-energy food and had flashlights. But they had only one sleeping bag among them and no snow shovels, tents, stoves or radio signaling devices. They were adequately prepared for a spring-weather climb and had no reason to suspect they should have carried cold-weather survival gear. But even if they didn't have all the optimum equipment, they had something even more important. They had their wits about them, and they had knowledge of how to survive cold-weather emergencies.

"We made a mistake and ended up not checking our compass soon enough," said one of the survivors. "After about three hours of going in the wrong direction, we tried to correct our direciton with the compass and then with a map."

By that time, night was falling and they were still above timberline. They found shelter under a rock outcropping. To retain their body heat, they made maximum use of their two space blankets and one sleeping bag; two of them crowded into the bag and one wrapped up in the blankets, changing positions every hour. "Saturday night and Sunday morning were pretty miserable, but we never thought we were not going to get through it" said a survivor.

The next day, well over a hundred searchers ventured into the raging storm searching for any trace of the missing team. But visibility was seldom more than a few yards, and the searchers had to devote much of their energy to protecting themselves from the severe conditions. And helicopters were not even able to get near the mountain because visibility was so limited. Just before dark, three sets of tracks which were possibly the missing team's were spotted well off the normal descent route; search leaders planned to divert some of their resources to that area the following morning.

Meanwhile, the missing team made it down to the 4,000-foot elevation, where they found shelter among trees, built a fire, dried out their wet clothing, and got a good night's sleep. (*Warm* and *Dry:* the two imperatives for survival.) The following day, just before noon, the three were spotted by a rescue helicopter, which picked them up and flew them back up (!) to their waiting friends and relatives at Timberline Lodge.

"We were hoping to walk right to Timberline Lodge so nobody would have to search for us any more," said one of the climbers. "But I'm glad we got the helicopter ride. It was pretty fun."

His climbing partner commented, "Maybe things worked out as well as they did because we've climbed together before and know each other well. We were able to talk through things. He's a pretty cool cookie."

A cool cookie, who knows the importance of staying *warm!*

APPENDIX I
MECHANICAL HELP

This book is focused on the use of insulation to maintain natural body warmth. This section lists some mechanical devices for those who want the extra help they provide. These devices are not necessary for warmth when an adequate insulation system is used. They are short-term devices which are not capable of providing more than a few hours of help in specific areas. They should NOT be relied on for serious warmth in most outdoor situations.

Electrified mittens and socks: These devices use batteries to provide warmth for the hands or feet for four to five hours. The socks come with the battery pack attached, or on a cord to be placed in your pocket or pack. Be sure that the socks fit your boot-sock combination and that they won't constrict your circulation.

Hand warmers: The older devices used either solid-fuel sticks or lighter fuel poured inside. They may contain asbestos, so it's best to steer clear of them unless you know they're asbestos-free. The newer versions are plastic packets of chemicals which slowly give off heat when activated by the user. They come in different sizes, for more or less heat. They are mostly throw-away items, but a reusable version also is available.

Kerosene or gasoline heaters: These devices are dangerous for a number of reasons: they pose a threat of fire hazard which has claimed more than a few lives; they have caused death by asphyxiation; they always have the potential for exploding; and handling their fuel in very low temperatures carries the threat of severe frostbite. You can always add more insuation to stay warm, no matter how cold it gets. The use of these stoves is far too great a risk to make them worthwhile.

APPENDIX II
FUTURE POSSIBILITIES

Research and development of new ideas for staying warm in cold environments continue at a brisk pace. The markets for warm clothing are quite lucrative in some parts of the country, and many government agencies also have a vested interest in keeping their personnel warm in cold environments.

Synthetic Down

Private industry, supplemented by government-backed research, has been searching for years to find an alternative to down insulation which would be lighter than current synthetics and possibly warmer. In at least two cases, results have been positive and may wind up being the new challenge to down. One of the new insulations is, like down, blown into pockets sewn between fabric layers; the other has been fabricated into batts like other synthetics.

The American Hoechst Co. calls their new down-like insulation *Universe*. The fiber used is a polyester with a special cross-section. It is blown into the garment, just as with down. Initial use (as is usual with most new insulations) was in pillows, where it has been enthusiastically received. Sleeping bags with the material are currently being tested. Critical factors will be the material's ability to regain its loft after being compressed, its loft-power for its weight, its loft after wetting and its longevity. (Loft helps determine a material's thermal-resistivity.)

The other new batt-fabricated insulation is actually a group of different insulations researched by the Albany International Research Co., with much of the work done under contract for the Army's Natick Research Center. Three different groups of fiber combinations were studied; two of these appear to have great potential. These synthetic combinations are stronger under compression than down, have about equal resilience, retain loft better when wet and are extremely close to down in thermal efficiency on a unit-weight basis. If the testing of clothing made from this batting is as positive as the original development work, the Army has a winner here. The taxpayers could benefit greatly from this research when and if private manufacturers start using the new material.

New Foams

The plastics industry regularly experiments with new compounds, and new foams are always being created. Some of them may be useful as insulation for homes; some in clothing, sleeping bags and pads. One promising new compound being developed is *Aerogel.* It is translucent, so it perhaps could be used as window insulation. In one form, it has an R-20 insulating value per inch; this makes it 2.5 times better than best commercial insulation now available. If it's ever perfected to the point of being transparent, our future windows will be warmer than our present walls! A principal use of this solid foam by campers, climbers and spelunkers is as emergency equipment for slowing conductive heat-loss between the user and the ground.

Phase-Change Chemicals

Research is being done using special heat-absorbing chemicals embedded in clothing. These compounds actually change phase and absorb heat as your body gives it off; when you cool down, they return heat to you slowly as they change back to their original phase. With these compounds, you could conserve heat and prevent getting chilled by cooling down too fast or too much. Whether these compounds can be incorporated into cloth in a way that will last, be efficient for the weight and also be cost-effective, remains to be seen.

Bagless Tents

The Army is using tents that have multiple layers of fabric in the canopy, with about ⅜-inch spacing between the layers. This creates dead-air spaces which insulate the tent. If enough layers are used, the occupants can be warm enough to sleep without sleeping bags (warmed just by their own body-heat). This is not a new idea; it was first used by Jack Stephenson in his *Air-gap* tents in the early 70's. Production eventually stopped due to high costs, but the concept remains valid. If inexpensive manufacturing methods can be developed, this type of tent may once again be viable for civilian use.

Ballistice-Cloth Outer Shell

The two strongest fibers used for cloth today are *Kevlar* by DuPont and *Spectra Fiber* by Allied Fibers. They are used to make sails, bulletproof vests, chaps (leggings that protect against chainsaw cuts, rattlesnake bites, etc.) and gloves designed to protect the hands from sharp objects. This type of cloth would be the ultimate outer layer of clothing. It would still require a waterprooof/windproof layer (such as *Gore-tex* from W L Gore) or coating (such as *Seal-Coat* from Patagonia), but the ballistics-cloth would provide protection from brush, thickets and thorns, as well as animal claws and teeth. It would also not rip apart from arctic ice, sharp rocks or a 100-plus mph wind. When and if the price of these fibers comes down a bit, they will make one helluva parka!

APPENDIX III

SOURCES OF WARM CLOTHING

Acquiring reliably warm clothing can be quick and easy, or it can present quite a challenge. Much depends on where you begin. Obviously, the selection will be far greater in Wisconsin or Maine than in Florida or Hawaii. Those who live in warmer regions may have to shop by mail, or wait until they are near or at their cold weather destination, before finding a reasonable selection.

Cost is another consideration. More expensive doesn't always mean warmer; but unusually inexpensive garments are seldom the warmest. Careful shopping and selection can usually turn up warmth-effective clothing at reasonable prices. But, before succumbing to bargain prices, consider whether the dollars saved are worth the cost (and pain) of treatment for hypothermia, frostbite, etc.!

Where I live there are many sources of warm clothing nearby; covering the spectrum from very cheap to ridiculously expensive. I have spent many hours closely comparing their offerings, learning quite a bit in the process. I've also been well satisfied with the clothing purchased through catalogs; again I've been able to learn quite a bit from the catalogs themselves.

Unfortunately, the advice of those selling warm garments cannot always be trusted. It is not that the salesclerks are dishonest, rather they often have had little or no first-hand experience with the clothing in really cold conditions. So it is imperative that you do your homework BEFORE you shop, and that you carefully plan just how you will combine various garments to form effective layers under the coldest conditions you may reasonably (or, unreasonably!) anticipate.

Outdoor Specialty Stores and Chains:

These generally offer the broadest selection of good to highest quality goods. Prices may be a bit higher than elsewhere, but they typically offer the very latest technologies, and their salespeople are much more apt to be active users of the gear they sell. The larger chains, such as Recreational Equipment Incorporated (REI), Eastern Mountain Sports, The North Face, Eddie Bauer, etc., have retail outlets in most major metropolitan areas; many also produce highly informative catalogs. If you are short on time and/or self confidence, these stores are likely your best choice.

Catalog Outlets:

These range from round-the-clock retailers such as L L Bean to someone selling "irregulars or seconds" and manufacturers' closeouts from a storage unit through a Post Office box. Their catalog can provide fascinating reading, and frequent bargains on discontinued models. Compare the offerings from several catalogs, decide what you think you need, then read the catalog descriptions again, including ALL the fine print! Be sure you understand the cataloger's returns policy (if any) before you order. And if in doubt on sizes, order the next largest, keeping in mind that you may want to add additional layers beneath it.

Discount Chains:

Selection is usually very limited and often very seasonal. Clerks are rarely knowledgeable, but prices can be good. You must really do your homework BEFORE shopping in these places.

Ski Shops:

These tend to be concentrated in or near those major metropolitan areas within reasonable driving distance of downhill ski areas, or at the areas themselves. They will usually feature the very latest in high-style clothing, and generally have high-style prices to match. But they typically attempt to clear their entire clothing inventory before the end of each ski season; some bargains may be had during such sales. Color-blindness helps!

Army/Navy "Surplus" Stores:

These can provide an interesting experience, but require very savvy shopping. At one time genuine "'Mickey Mouse" boots could be found in such establishments for a pittance; now the best you can expect is a questionable imitation. Always ask yourself two questions: why is this merchandise "surplus"? and which Army (or Navy) originally designed it?

Bicycle Shops:

Perhaps the best place to begin if biking is your principal planned activity. The clerks almost always use what they sell (check for bugs on their teeth when they smile!) and prices tend to be competitive.

Marine Supply Houses:

If you are fortunate enough to live in or near a major seaport, check out those shops that cater to professional mariners; look along the "working waterfront." The clothing will likely be very rugged and functional, with little attention paid to styling. Prices should generally be reasonable, and salespeople very knowledgeable.

If your region lacks these "industrial grade" shops, try those catering to the recreational boater. Styling will be much better, prices perhaps higher, but check carefully for durability and functionality.

Most shops specializing in canoes and/or kayaks also carry a good selection of clothing specifically designed for these activities. Often, such clothing will function just as well when worn ashore, and can provide versatile additions to your outdoor wardrobe.

Department Stores:

Emphasis tends to be more on clothing that looks good and appears to be warm. But some very good bargains may be had at season-ending sales.

Thrift Shops:

Worth checking out, especially if the budget is tight. Surprisingly, some of the best bargains are to be had where the weather is warmest; someone transferred from Detroit to Dallas may just have cleaned out his closet...!

Garage Sales:

If you stop for such signs anyway, you just may find something usable and at a bargain price. Selection (and prices) may be best in the spring and summer, when bulky clothing takes up valuable closet space. Good luck!

APPENDIX IV
FURTHER READING

Hypothermia: Death by Exposure by William W Forgey, MD; 1985, ICS Books, Merriville, Indiana

Hypothermia, Frostbite, and other Cold Injuries; James A Wilkerson, MD, Editor, 1986, The Mountaineers, Seattle

Hypothermia: Killer of the Unprepared by Theodore G Lathrop, MD, 1972, Mazamas, Portland, Oregon

Frostbite by Bradford Washburn, Museum of Science, Boston

Backpacking, One Step at a Time by Harvey Manning, Recreational Equipment, Inc., Seattle

Winter Hiking and Camping by John A Danielson, 1972, Adirondak Mountain Club, Glens Falls, New York

Keeping Warm and Dry by Harry Roberts, 1982, Stone Wall Press, Washington, DC

Snow Camping and Mountaineering by Edward A Rossit, 1974, Funk and Wagnalls, New York

The Complete Snow Camper's Guide by Raymond Bridge, 1973, Scribner's, New York

Wilderness Skiing by Lito Tejada-Flores and Allen Steck, 1972, Sierra Club, San Francisco

Surviving the Unexpected Wilderness Emergency by Gene Fear, 1972, Survival Education Association, Tacoma, Washington

Mountaineering- Freedom of the Hills; The Mountaineers, Seattle

The Wilderness Handbook by Paul Petzoldt, 1974, Norton, New York

The Book of Survival by Anthony Greenbank, 1967, Harper and Row, New York

INDEX

THE MOUNTAINEERS, founded in 1906, is a nonprofit outdoor activity and conservation club, whose mission is "to explore, study, preserve, and enjoy the natural beauty of the outdoors{4ell}" Based in Seattle, Washington, the club is now the third-largest such organization in the United States, with 15,000 members and five branches throughout Washington State.

The Mountaineers sponsors both classes and year-round outdoor activities in the Pacific Northwest, which include hiking, mountain climbing, ski-touring, snowshoeing, bicycling, camping, kayaking and canoeing, nature study, sailing, and adventure travel. The club's conservation division supports environmental causes through educational activities, sponsoring legislation, and presenting informational programs. All club activities are led by skilled, experienced volunteers, who are dedicated to promoting safe and responsible enjoyment and preservation of the outdoors.

If you would like to participate in these organized outdoor activities or the club's programs, consider a membership in The Mountaineers. For information and an application, write or call The Mountaineers, Club Headquarters, 300 Third Avenue West, Seattle, Washington 98119; (206) 284-6310.

The Mountaineers Books, an active, nonprofit publishing program of the club, produces guidebooks, instructional texts, historical works, natural history guides, and works on environmental conservation. All books produced by The Mountaineers are aimed at fulfilling the club's mission.

Send or call for our catalog of more than 300 outdoor titles:

The Mountaineers Books
1001 SW Klickitat Way, Suite 201
Seattle, WA 98134
1-800-553-4453
e-mail: mbooks@mountaineers.org
website: www.mountaineers.org